HANDBOOK OF IRIS

HANDBOOK OF IRISH CASE LAW 1984

EXTRACTED FROM

Irish Law Reports Monthly

WITH AN

INTRODUCTION

BY

Eamonn Cahill B.A. Barrister-at-Law

THE ROUND HALL PRESS
DUBLIN

This book was typeset for the Round Hall Press Ltd., Kill Lane, Blackrock, Co. Dublin (Telephone 850922) by Ree Pro Ltd, Dublin.

© Introduction and Reports: The Round Hall Press Ltd., 1984.

All rights reserved. No part of this publication may be reproduced, stored in a retrieval system, or transmitted in any form, or by any means, electronic, mechanical, photocopying, recording or otherwise, without the prior permission of The Round Hall Press Ltd.

Printed in Ireland.

ISBN 0 9508725 3 9

PREFACE

Last year we published the *Student Law Reporter 1983* which covered all the judgments reported in *Irish Law Reports Monthly* of the previous year. This 1984 edition has been given the new title of *Handbook of Irish Case Law*: we have become aware that it is helpful not only to students of law and related subjects but also to legal practitioners, accountants, civil servants, banks etc. The handbook has been specially prepared for quick and easy reference and the general subject matter contents page will be of particular help where the case name has slipped the memory.

As in its predecessor, *Handbook of Irish Case Law* covers judgments that were reported in *Irish Law Reports Monthly* for the previous year — in this case 1983. From a glance at the list of cases reported in the Subject Index one can see the range of cases covered. 1983, incidentally, produced a higher number of judgments than in average years.

The judgments emanate from the Supreme, High and Circuit Courts of Ireland together with selected cases from the Employment Appeals Tribunal.

In the Introduction to this handbook Eamonn Cahill, BL, reviews the principles of law and the impact these cases have had on them. The judgments cover a wide range of subjects including injunctions, practice, local government, tort, constitutional, patents, licensing, family and labour law.

For detailed study purposes students are referred to the full texts of the judgments reported in [1983] *Irish Law Reports Monthly*.

Bart D. Daly, Editor
ILRM
1 August 1984

ABBREVIATIONS

AC	Appeal Cases
All ER	All England Law Reports 1936–
ALJR	Australian Law Journal Reports 1958–
ALT	American Law Times 1868-77
Ad and El	Adolphus & Ellis Reports 1834-40
Amb	Ambler's Chancery Reports 1737-84
App Cas	Appeal Cases
B & S	Best & Smith's Queen's Bench Reports (121-2 ER) 1861–5
B & S	Beven & Siefel's Ceylon Reports (Sri. L. 1859–75)
CA	Court of Appeal
CAR	Civil Air Regulations (USA)
CB	Common Bench Reports 1845-56
CU(NS)	California Unreported Cases
Ch D	Law Reports, Chancery Division 1876-90
Ch	Chancery Court of Division
Coke Rep.	Coke's King's Bench Reports 1572-1616
Cowp	Cowper's King's Bench Reports 1774-8
EG	Estates Gazette
EHRR	European Human Rights Reports 1979-
E and B	Ellis & Blackburn 1846-1866
El & Bl	Ellis & Blackburn's Queen Bench Reports 1851-8
Exch	Exchequer Reports 1847-56
FSR	Fleet Street Reports
Hob	Hobart's King's Bench Reports 1603-25
ICLR	Irish Common Law Reports 2nd Series 1850-66
ICR	Industrial Court Reports
ILRM	Irish Law Reports Monthly 1981–
ILTR	Irish Law Times Reports
IR	Irish Reports
IRLR	Industrial Relations Law Reports
Ir Ch R	Irish Chancery Reports 1850-66
Ir Jur Rep	Irish Jurist Reports 1935-6
JP	Justice of the Peace
KB	King's Bench
L.J. Ch	Law Journal Reports, Chancery New Series 1831-46
LJ Ex	Law Journal Reports, Exchequer, New Series 1831-75
LR Exch	Law Reports, Exchequer 1865-75
LR Ir	Law Reports, Ireland 1878-93
LR	Law Reports 1865–
LR/HL	Law Reports, English & Irish Appeals 1866-75
LR, Sc & Div	Law Reports, Scotch and Divorce Appeals 1866-75
Ld Ray	Lord Raymond 1694-1732
M & W	Meeson & Welsby's Exchequer Reports 1836-47
Mod	Modern Law Reports 1669-1755
NW	North Western Reporter (USA)
P & CR	Planning and Compensation Reports 1949–
PD	Perry & Davison's Queen's Bench Reports (48-54RR) 1838-41
PD	Probate & Divorce
QB	Law Reports, Queen's Bench 1891–
QBD	Law Reports, Queen's Bench Division 1875-90
RPC	Reports of Patent, Design & Trade Mark Cases 1884–
Sim	Simons (1826-1852)

TC	Reports of Tax Cases 1875–
TLR	Times Law Reports 1884-1952
Taunt	Taunt's Common Pleas Reports
US	United States Supreme Court Reports 1790–
WLR	Weekly Law Reports
WWR	Western Weekly Reports (Can.) (1911-50) 1955–

OTHER

Cases with ET or DEP or EAT	Refers to Employment Appeals Tribunal determinations.
Nem. Diss (in case title)	(Nemine dissentiente) No one dissenting.
Date in title	Date of delivery of judgment

CASES REPORTED

ILRM Citation [1983]			Page
		ADOPTION	
228	HC	McF v G & G, The Sacred Heart Adoption Society and the Adoption Board	25
		COMPANY	
323	HC	In the Matter of Clubman Shirts Ltd; and In the Matter of the Companies Acts, 1963 to 1977; and In the Matter of ss.205 and 371 of the Companies Act 1963	26
329	SC	The Revenue Commissioners v Donnelly	27
503	HC	Continental Irish Meat Ltd (in Receivership and in Voluntary Liquidation) v the Minister for Agriculture	28
510	HC	In the Matter of Pageboy Couriers Ltd., and In the Matter of the Companies Act 1963 to 1982	29
516	HC	Patrick McGowan and Others and (by order) Food Products (Donegal) Ltd v Joseph Gannon	30
		COMPULSORY PURCHASE	
56	HC	Gunning v Dublin Corporation	31
		CONSTITUTION	
52	HC	The State (Whelan) v the Governor of Mountjoy Prison	32
67	HC	McCann v the Attorney General and The Racing Board	33
79	SC	O'Sullivan v Hartnett, the Attorney General and Ireland	34
89	SC	The State (Lynch) v Patrick Cooney, Minister for Posts and Telegraphs and Another	35
246	SC	Re Reference Under Article 26 of the Constitution of the Housing (Private Rented Dwellings) Bill 1981	37

314	SC	O'Brien v Bord na Mona and the Attorney General	38
391	HC	O'Callaghan v The Commissioners of Public Works in Ireland and Others	39
429	HC	Mark Cooke (An Infant, Suing by his Father and Next Friend William Cooke) v Walsh	42
449	HC	Brennan and Others v the Attorney General and Wexford County Council	44
489	HC	Costello v DPP and Another	47
549	SC	The People (DPP) v O'Shea	48

CRIMINAL LAW

17	SC	State (Aherne) v The Governor of Limerick Prison	50
45	HC	State (Delaney) v District Justice Magee and Others	52
76	SC	DPP v Clein	53
149	SC	State (Rogers) v Galvin	53
169	SC	McGlinchey v Wren	54
237	CCA	DPP v Kehoe	55
241	HC	State (O'Hagan) v District Justice Sean Delap	56
271	SC	DPP v Kelly	57
285	HC	State (Williams) v DPP and District Justice Kelleher	59
291	SC	State (Laffey) v His Hon. Judge John Grattan Esmonde, DPP and Another	61
310	HC	State (Higgins) v Reid	61
355	HC	In the Matter of an Application by Malcolm MacArthur	62
411	HC	DPP v McPartland	63
525	HC	State (McDonagh) v District Justice J. Barry	64
537	SC	State (Williams) v DPP and Kelleher	65
591	SC	People (DPP) v O'Shea	67

FAMILY LAW

380	HC	CP v DP	67
387	HC	S v S	68

INJUNCTIONS

254	SC	The Attorney General at the Relation of Francis X Martin v Dublin Corporation and The Commissioners of Public Works in Ireland	69

258	HC	Campus Oil Ltd and Others v the Minister for Industry and Energy, Ireland, The A.G. and Another	70
541	HC	Fleming and Others v Ranks (Ireland) Ltd and Another	72

INTERNATIONAL LAW

163	HC	O'Daly and Reverte v Gulf Oil Terminals (Ireland) Ltd and Others	73

LABOUR LAW

50	CC	IBM v Feeney	74
363	EAT	Lewis v Squash Ireland Ltd	75

LANDLORD & TENANT

532	HC	Enock and Leon Hairstylist Ltd v Lambert Jones Estates Ltd and Sydney Vard Ltd	76

LICENSING

41	HC	DPP v O'Toole	77

NATURAL JUSTICE

331	SC	State (Williams) v Army Pensions Board and the Minister for Defence	78
407	HC	State (at the Prosecution of Hussey) v Irish Land Commission and Others	79

NEGLIGENCE

429	HC	Cooke v Walsh	42
595	HC	Cole v Webb Caravans Ltd and Another	80

PATENTS

500	SC	Beecham Group Ltd v Bristol Myers Company	81

PLANNING

1	SC	Crodaun Homes Ltd v Kildare County Council	82
12	HC	State (Genport Ltd) v An Bord Pleanala	83
48	HC	Dublin Corporation v Maiden Poster Sites Ltd	83

125	HC	State (Flynn & O'Flaherty Ltd) v Dublin Corporation	84
141	HC	O'Neill v Clare County Council	85
145	SC	State (Magauran) v Dublin Corporation	85
213	HC	Byrne v Dublin County Council	86
268	HC	Carrick Hall Holdings Ltd v Dublin Corporation	88
339	SC	Creedon v Dublin Corporation	89
377	SC	Dublin County Council v Shortt	90
413	HC	Gammell v Dublin County Council	91

PRACTICE & PROCEDURE

7	HC	Magauran v Dargan and Dargan and Partner Ltd	92
152	HC	Mellowhide Products Ltd v Barry Agencies Ltd	93
350	HC	Chemical Bank v Peter McCormack	94
507	HC	Reen v Bank of Ireland Finance Ltd and Luceys Garage (Mallow) Ltd	95

REVENUE

| 34 | HC | Revenue Commissioners v O'Reilly and Another, Trustees of Club 349 | 96 |

ROAD TRAFFIC ACT

| 223 | SC | DPP (Long) v McDonald and Others and O'Mahony and Others v Biggs and Others | 97 |
| 429 | HC | Cooke v Walsh | 42 |

SALE OF GOODS

| 402 | HC | In the Matter of the Companies Act 1963 and In the Matter of Galway Concrete Ltd (In liquidation) | 98 |

SALE OF LAND

82	HC	Crean v Drinan	100
206	SC	Roberts v O'Neill and Another	101
295	HC	Keating and Others v Bank of Ireland and Others	102
343	SC	Weir v Somers	103
513	HC	Crowley v Flynn	105

STATUTE OF LIMITATIONS

128	SC	Bellew v Bellew and Bellew	106
156	HC	Morgan v Park Developments Ltd	107
300	HC	Smith v Ireland, the Attorney General & Another	108

SUCCESSION

519	HC	MH and N McG v NM and CM	110

TORT

112	SC	Adidas v O'Neill & Co. Ltd	111
173	HC	CIE v Carroll and Wexford County Council	112
186	SC	O'Dowd v North Western Health Board	114

WILLS

359	HC	In the Matter of the Will of Antonie Marie Bonnet, deceased: Robert William Roche Johnston v Heinz H. Langheld & Others and (by order) the Representative Church Body	116

INTRODUCTION

The introduction to the *Handbook of Irish Case Law* seeks to review those judgments most likely to contribute to the re-assessment of principles of law long regarded as inimitable.

The third volume of the *Irish Law Reports Monthly* contains quite a large number of cases that have major constitutional indications. The Constitution of Ireland guarantees in a positive manner the existence of certain 'fundamental rights' comprised chiefly in Articles 40 to 44 of the Constitution of 1937. These rights relate to personal liberty, integrity, freedom of expression and of course property rights.

The Constitution is seen by the courts as a guarantor against unjust encroachments by the State on the liberties of the citizens in both their individual and collective capacities. The role of the judiciary is also constitutionally guaranteed. In Articles 34 to 38, which deal with the administration of justice, the independence of the judicial power is guaranteed against encroachment by the legislature.

The provisions of Article 34 confirm that the Supreme Court and the High Court have the jurisdiction to determine questions concerning the validity of any act of the Oireachtas without qualification or condition. The courts regard themselves as the ultimate guarantors of citizens' rights under the Constitution. In defining the fundamental rights of the citizen the Constitution as interpreted by the courts also ensures that the administration of justice must be conducted with basic fairness of procedures. The Superior Courts have the jurisdiction to review procedures of lower courts, i.e. the Circuit Court and the District Court, when complainants allege that there was less than fairness in the determining of their cases. The procedure involved consists of submissions by the interested parties when the complaint is analysed in accordance with the constitutional guarantees as interpreted through the increasing case-loads of such matters.

The first case under review is the *State (Delaney) v District Justice Sean Magee & Ors*. In this case the prosecutor was convicted in the District Court of drunken driving contrary to s. 49 of the Road Traffic Act, 1961 as amended. Delaney was sentenced to three months imprisonment and a fine of £250 with a further six months in prison in default of payment. The accused as prosecutor submitted that the order of the District Court rendered him liable to serve a total prison sentence of nine months and that this was therefore in excess of jurisdiction. The maximum permissible sentence for an offence under s. 49 is six months imprisonment. The prosecutor obtained from Barrington J an order of certiorari which would in effect have quashed the order of the District Court unless cause should be shown to the contrary. When cause was shown by the respondents Gannon J allowed the cause shown and discharged the conditional order of certiorari. After reviewing the submissions made by the prosecutor Gannon J held that the several enactments (including s. 3 of the Criminal Justice Administration Act, 1914 and Rule 65 of the District Court Rules for scales of imprisonment proportioned to amounts of fines) indicate that the two imprisonment sentences are of quite different character and that therefore there was no excess of jurisdiction in the District Court order.

In prosecutions under the Road Traffic Acts it is always encumbent upon the State to show that all of the statutory proofs have been complied with. It is no surprise that there are probably more State Side applications brought under the Road Traffic Act, 1961 to 1978 than under any other single statute enacted since the foundation of the State. *The Director of Public Prosecution v Stuart Clein* was a consultative case stated from the District Court which came before the High Court for a ruling on a legal submission made on the defendant's behalf that two summonses served on him to appear in the District Court on charges of refusing and failing to comply with the provisions of ss. 12(2) and 13(3) of the Road Traffic (Amendment) Act, 1978 were invalid. Neither of the two summonses was served in time for the hearing in the District Court which was subsequently adjourned to a later date. Before they were re-served the date of issue was altered and initialled by the peace commissioner who had issued the summonses. Both the complainant and the defendant were represented when the summonses were called. After a number of further adjournments the District Justice proceeded to hear the summonses. At the conclusion of the prosecution's case the defendant, who did not offer any evidence, asked the District Justice to state a case to the High Court. In the High Court Gannon J held that the amended summonses had been served within six months of the making of the complaints. While he was satisfied that the defendant had not shown that service of the summonses had been defective, he went on to say that, even if there had been a procedural breach, such a breach would have been cured when the defendant appeared (as he did appear) in the District Court on the day specified in the summons for hearing.

In another case stated, *The State (Christopher Aherne) v The Governor of Limerick Prison*, the Supreme Court was asked to decide on the question of whether a Circuit Court Judge can oppose an increased sentence on an appeal from the District Court where the Notice of Appeal relates to conviction only and no reference is made to the sentence imposed in the District Court. The prosecutor, Christopher Aherne, had been sentenced in Cork District Court to nine months imprisonment. He appealed against conviction only and the Circuit Court Judge affirmed the sentence and increased it to 12 months imprisonment. Aherne then brought certiorari proceedings in the High Court where he was granted a conditional order under Article 40.4.2º of the Constitution on the grounds that the Circuit Court Judge did not have the necessary jurisdiction to increase the sentence. Upon the respondent showing cause the matter was heard before Gannon J. The prosecutor (Christopher Aherne) argued that the procedure provided in the District Court Rules permitted an appeal against conviction only and that as the appeal was limited to conviction only the Circuit Court Judge had no jurisdiction to increase the District Court sentence. This argument was sustained in the High Court and Gannon J quashed the Circuit Court order. Upon an appeal the Supreme Court unanimously agreed that the Circuit Court did have the jurisdiction to increase a sentence on an appeal against conviction only. Walsh J and Griffin J pointed out that an appeal of the District Court is by way of re-trial which enables the possibility of a totally different case being made by either or both sides and by the time the appeal takes place the evidence may reveal a more aggravated case than had appeared in the District Court. In addition Walsh J held that the re-trial in the Circuit Court commences on the assumption that the accused is innocent until he is proven guilty on the re-trial and that it would appear unusual if he starts off a new trial with sentence already determined.

The Extradition Act, 1965, s. 47 has frequently been relied on as a ground for appealing extradition orders made in the District Court. S. 47 provides that the High Court may make a direction for the release of the person ordered to be detained if, *inter alia*, the offence with which he is charged is a political one or it is an offence connected with a political motive. In the case of *Dominic McGlinchy v Commissioner Laurence Wrenn* the Supreme Court was asked by the prosecutor, Dominic McGlinchy, to set aside the High Court order of Gannon J who had refused the order sought for his release following an extradition order made in the District Court. In an affidavit grounding his claim McGlinchy swore that the offence with which he had been charged and for which he was being extradited was a political offence or an offence connected with a political offence. The Extradition Act does not define exactly what constitutes a political offence and the Supreme Court is required to decide on the facts of each particular case to see if the offence in question constitutes a political one. In reviewing the exhibits O'Higgins CJ noted that the plaintiff was alleged to have murdered an elderly woman in what he regarded as revolting and cowardly circumstances. In a passage which may well presage the Supreme Court's attitude to further extradition appeals O'Higgins CJ indicated that in his view the judicial authorities relied upon in defining the political nature of such offences have in many respects been rendered obsolete by the fact that modern terrorist violence is often the very antithesis of what could reasonably be regarded as political. The court rejected the appeal and in doing so it was seen to have established new guidelines of approach in considering s. 47 of the Act. An analysis of the Chief Justice's judgment would appear to put a greater onus on the applicant to show that both the offence and the motivation behind it must come within the rather narrowly confined parameters of the Chief Justice's definition of political activity.

In the criminal law the plea of *autrefois acquit* is a long established defence to any attempt to recharge an accused who has already been found not guilty of the same offence. In the case of *The People* (*DPP*) *v Patrick Leo O'Shea* the accused O'Shea was found not guilty of certain offences in the Central Criminal Court. While the jury reached a verdict of not guilty they did so, however, on the direction of the trial judge. The Director of Public Prosecution then appealed to the Supreme Court against the trial judge. The Supreme Court was required to consider two questions. Firstly, does an appeal lie at the suit of the Director of Public Prosecutions to the Supreme Court against a verdict of not guilty reached by a jury in the Central Criminal Court? This in turn raised a separate issue of whether or not Article 34.4.3º of the Constitution allows the Supreme Court to entertain appeals from all decisions of the High Court other than those specifically provided by statute. While Article 34.4.3º states that the Supreme Court's appellate jurisdiction over the High Court extends 'from all decisions of that Court', the central issue became whether or not the words 'from all decisions of the High Court' should be given a restrictive or a universal interpretation.

The court drew the distinction between the verdicts arrived at in the Central Criminal Court which were by direction of the trial judge and those similar verdicts properly arrived at by a jury who had not been so directed who considered all of the evidence and then decided the issue on the merits.

The Supreme Court held that there was nothing in the Constitution to qualify the provisions of Article 34.4.3º that all decisions of the High Court, except those specifically provided for, may be appealed to the Supreme Court. O'Higgins CJ also held that appeals would not lie from verdicts of acquittal properly arrived at by a jury which had decided on the merits of the case. However, in dissenting judgments Finlay P and Henchy J felt that the right to a trial by a jury as provided by the Constitution includes the right to a trial with a jury and that an essential characteristic of such a right is that a jury's verdict of 'not guilty' is not subject to appeal by any other court. Finlay P felt that the statutory enactments since the passing of s. 34 of the Courts of Justice Act, 1924 specify the grounds on which criminal appeals can be made by the State in a manner that was sufficient to enable him to conclude that the legislature had accepted that an accused was immune from further prosecution once a favourable decision had been reached in his case. Finlay P continued that in perusing the decisions of Irish courts over the past 100 years there was not one single instance of a decision by a court at any level that an appeal lay on the acquittal of a person on a criminal charge with a jury.

The Supreme Court was faced with an appeal from the Special Criminal Court in the first ever prosecution under s. 7 of the Offences Against the State Act, 1939 as amended by s. 2 of the Criminal Law Act, 1976. In the *Director of Public Prosecutions v Kehoe* the accused appealed against a sentence imposed in the Special Criminal Court where he had been charged with obstruction of Government. The court heard evidence that the accused had taken part in an anti-H-Block demonstration outside the British Embassy. Kehoe was found guilty and sentenced to two years imprisonment. The word 'Government', as it is referred to in s. 1(7) of the Offences Against the State Act, is given a broader meaning than the sense in which it is used in Article 28 of the Constitution. In s. 7 it is recognised that 'Government' may include any of its concomatant branches, whether legislative, judicial or executive, and this can include the Gardaí and the military powers of the State. The court failed to define the precise type of conduct contemplated by s. 7 but concluded nonetheless that to constitute an offence under the section it is necessary that the offence with which an accused has been charged must constitute an attack on the State through one of its constitutent organs, be it a judge, a member of the Oireachtas or a member of the Garda Síochána. Unlike s. 9 of the Act it is not necessary that intent to undermine public order should be proved. The terms of the section apply to the prevention or obstruction by violence of the exercise or performance of any one of the constitutent arms of the Government or any of its branches.

FAMILY LAW

Two family law cases were reported in ILRM [1983]. In *C.P. v D.P.* the court was asked to consider the implications involved in the construction of s. 5(1) of the Family Home Protection Act, 1976. In this case the defendant husband deposited the title deeds of the family home with a bank as security for an overdraft. The plaintiff wife did not give consent to the deposit. She claimed that the defendant had deposited the title deeds without her consent as security for a number of overdrafts. She then alleged that her husband was engaging in such conduct as may lead to the loss of the family home with the presumed intention of depriving her and her dependent children of their residence in it. It was also suggested further that the word 'intention' in the sub-section should be construed as not being equivalent with motive, but rather with the 'intention' which may be imputed to any person as to the natural and probable consequences of their conduct. This submission, however, was rejected by Finlay J who held that to establish necessary intention one must show that there was an element of deliberate conduct involved which would present a risk to the loss of an interest in the family home. In a similar case in *S v S* a plaintiff wife also sought an order under s. 5(1) of the Family Home Protection Act, 1976. In reviewing the evidence of the case McWilliam J commented that the defendant had looked after his family to the best of his ability, although largely on borrowed money. He continued that although the defendant had acted improvidentially and possibly dishonestly, well knowing that the family home might become a target for creditors; and he concluded that it was unlikely that the defendant had formed any intention of depriving his wife and children of their residence in the family home.

INJUNCTIONS

The law on injunctions in Ireland seems little changed from the principles enacted in the *Educational Company of Ireland v Fitzpatrick* [1961] IR 323. In what must be the most quoted judgment in the area of equitable relief in the Irish courts Lavery J cited with approval a passage on *Kerr on Injunctions* which suggested that a litigant seeking an interlocutory injunction 'must be able to show a fair *prima facie* case in support of the title which he asserts and that the court must be satisfied 'that the probabilities in favour of his (the defendant's) case ultimately failing in the final issue of the suit'. The judgment went on to say that 'the plaintiffs have to establish that there is a fair question raised to be decided at the trial'. English courts no longer require a probability that the plaintiff is entitled to a relief or that he should establish a strong *prima facie* case. It seems now that as a result of the *American Cyanamid Company v Ethicon Ltd* case that English courts will grant an injunction so long as the applicant can establish to the satisfaction of the court that his claim is neither frivolous nor vexatious. It was considered by most lawyers that the proofs required to obtain interlocutory relief in Irish courts place a greater onus on plaintiffs than was required by English courts. This distinction was highlighted to considerable effect by Murphy J in *Campus Oils Ltd and Ors v The Minister for Industry and Energy and Ors*. In this case the plaintiff sought interlocutory relief restraining the defendant from implementing the provisions of a ministerial order which empowered the Minister for Industry and Energy to determine the price of petroleum oil which the plaintiffs were required to purchase from the four defendants (The Irish National Petroleum Corporation Ltd) pending the determination of other proceedings. While the result of the *Cyanamid* case has been to make it easier to establish an entitlement to the relief claimed (in English courts), Diplock LJ a member of the court in that case agreed with Kingsmill Moore's judgment in the *Educational Company* case in observing that a court ought not to resolve a disputed question of face in anticipation of a plenary hearing. All of these factors were taken into consideration in the judgment of Murphy J who held that the distinction drawn between the judgments in the two cases are more apparent than real. He then referred to the commonality of views expressed by both Kingsmill Moore J and Lord Diplock in their respective judgments and in particular on how they approached the onus to be undertaken by an applicant for an interlocutory injunction.

Another case on the law of Injunctions is that of *Fleming v Ranks Ireland and Ors*. In this case the plaintiffs sought a Mareva injunction restraining the second defendant who was receiver of Ranks Ireland Ltd from disposing with the assets of the company. The grounds relied on were that Ranks were likely to dispose of some of its assets which consisted of flour so that any judgment obtained by the plaintiffs, would be worthless in any subsequent actions taken *inter partes*. S. 28(8) of the Judicature (Ireland) Act, 1888 confers jurisdiction on a court to grant interlocutory relief in all cases in which it should appear to be just or convenient that such an order should be made. In reviewing the law McWilliam J accepted that there must be a real risk of the removal or disposal of the defendant's assets and that there must also be a danger of default by the defendant and that of course the balance of convenience must be in favour of granting it.

He then concluded that a good case had been made on behalf of the plaintiffs and that the defendant did not deny its intention to dispose of the assets. However, it was denied in the defence that there was any intention of disposing of the assets to evade its obligations to the plaintiffs. This defence was sufficient for McWilliam J who decided that he would refuse the application. He contented himself with the observation that the court should abide by the Lister principle which is that an injunction will not be granted to restrain a defendant from parting with his assets so that they may be preserved in case the pltintiff's case succeeds. In reaching his conclusion the judge found himself in agreement with Sir Robert McGarry, VC in *Barclay/Johnson v Yuill* [1980] 1 WLR at 1259 who held that the Lister principle remains the rule, and that the Mareva doctrine constitutes a limited exception to it. 'The Lister Rules' refers to the case of *Lister & Co. v Stubbs* (1890) 445 ChD 1 where it was held that the court will not grant an injunction to restrain a defendant from parting with his assets so that they may be preserved in case the plaintiff's claim succeeds.

CONSTITUTIONAL

In recent years juries have become accustomed to awarding enormous sums of money in cases involving personal injuries. It has always been assumed that all of the damages awarded to successful litigants in such cases would have to be borne by the unsuccessful defendants or by their insurance companies, if they were insured. In *Mark Cooke (An Infant Suing by his Father and Next Friend William Cooke) v Patrick Walsh* a nine year old boy was so seriously injured in a road traffic accident that he will require constant medical supervision for the rest of his life. The infant plaintiff was awarded a sum in excess of £650,000. This award was made to cover and provide for his future financial loss of earnings and the cost of future care over a period of some 39 years which represented his life expectancy. The defendant's insurers argued that as the plaintiff was entitled to benefit free of charge on payment under the Health Act, 1970 the Local Health Board should be responsible for such charges. However, the plaintiff was ineligible for free services because of the provisions of the Health Services (Limited Eligibility Regulations) 1979. The defence then raised a constitutional point which challenged the validity of s. 72 of the Act. The trial judge, Hamilton J, held that s. 72 was not unconstitutional and that that section together with s. 56(2) and s. 52(1) has the effect of granting to the Minister for Health the power to exclude from health benefits a particular class of persons who would otherwise be eligible. He also held that the Minister was acting in accordance with the principles of constitutional justice. This case is under appeal to the Supreme Court and a reversal of the High Court decision will have very obvious and serious repercussions for all local health authoities.

In another constitutional action the High Court was asked to consider the constitutionality of the property valuation made under the Valuation Acts, 1852 to 1864. The plaintiffs, who were farmers from Co. Wexford, were members of an Association known as the 'P.L.V. Action Committee' under the auspices of the Wexford Branch of the Irish Farmers Association. For each of the plaintiffs the rateable valuation of their lands was based on that fixed during the primary valuation of lands in Ireland between 1853 and 1865 pursuant to the provisions of the Valuation (Ireland) Acts, 1856 to 1864. The rateable valuation determines the liabilities of each plaintiff farmer to pay income tax and rates upon their lands to their local county councils. The plaintiffs pleaded, *inter alia*, that the original valuation did not properly reflect the real value and productive capacity of any land on which valuations were fixed. They also pleaded that as a result of the valuations on their lands the latter were uneconomic and that the method of assessment constituted an unjust attack on their property rights contrary to Article 43 of the Constitution. They then sought a declaration that the Valuation Acts insofar as they provided for the valuation for rating purposes of agricultural lands within the State are inconsistent with the Constitution. In a comprehensive review of the highly technical evidence offered Barrington J concluded that it was not the fault of the Valuation Acts that their particular lands were wrongly valued when compared with the lands of farmers in other parts of the country. However, the Statute by denying the plaintiffs an effective means of having their lands valued through the absence of a proper appeal procedure was inconsistent with the Constitution.

LAW OF TORT

The tort of passing off is not a cause of action that is resorted to with any frequency in the Irish courts. In *Adidas v Charles O'Neill & Co Ltd*, the Adidas Sports Company claimed that an Irish company was guilty of passing off its sports wear as that of the plaintiffs. The plaintiffs were the proprietors of the famous three stripe design associated with their sports wear. Adidas had already secured the registration in Ireland of a trade mark consisting of three horizontal stripes on the side of the track suits. That trade mark, however, was not associated with every design of stripes on sports garments and the defendants countered the plaintiff's contention that they were passing off the goods as those of the plaintiff's good and argued that they had been using such a design for a substantial number of years. Another ground of the defence was that the three stripe design had acquired wide usage throughout the clothing trade. The claim was confined to the usage of a particular three stripe design to which the plaintiffs claimed an exclusive usage. In Kerley's *Law of Trade Marks*, 10th edition, it is related that 'There can hardly be passing off of any "get up" alone unless the resemblance between the goods is extremely close, so close that it can hardly occur except by deliberate imitation, and even that may not be enough'. In the High Court the plaintiff's claim failed on two grounds when McWilliam J held that they had not succeeded in establishing either an essential reputation in Ireland or that confusion had been caused by the defendant's use of the three stripe design. Adidas then appealed to the Supreme Court who divided two to one on the issue. O'Higgins CJ and Hederman J dismissed the appeal, while Henchy J reversed the High Court judgment. The latter expressed the opinion that Adidas had acquired a proprietary interest in the particular three stripe design. This view was in contrast with the majority decision which was that the plaintiffs had merely made the most of the demand for three stripes in sports wear. In Henchy J's judgment reference was made to the case of *C & A Modes v C & A Waterford Ltd* [1976] IR 197 where it was held that the plaintiff in such an action must show that the good will of proprietary interest in the symbol or get up in question was vested in him in this State at the time of the defendant's acts of which the plaintiff complained. After further review of the law, Henchy J indicated his satisfaction that the evidence in the case was coercive of the conclusion that Adidas had acquired outside Ireland an exclusive right to the use or get up. The remaining issue for him was whether such a right had been acquired in the State. Reliance was placed on Lord Justice Scarman's judgment in *Cadbury Schweppes v Pub Squash* [1981] 1 All ER 213 and the remaining test was whether Adidas had induced from advertising in the Irish market a distinctive character recognised by the market in this country. The conclusion he reached was in the affirmative.

ADOPTION

McF v G & G, The Sacred Heart Adoption Society and The Adoption Board: High Court 1980 No. 1008 Sp. (McWilliam J) 31 July 1981.

Adoption - Child placed for adoption - Consent form signed by mother - Subsequent delay - Allegation that mother pressurised to consent - Institution of proceedings by adoptive parents for order dispensing with the mother's consent - Whether consent freely given - Whether in child's best interests to remain with adoptive parents.

Facts The plaintiff sought an order for the return of her son born 16 May 1979 who had been in the custody of the first and second named defendants since August 1979. The infant was the plaintiff's second child, her first child having already been placed for adoption. The plaintiff later married and gave birth to a third child. The evidence disclosed that after its birth the plaintiff considered keeping the second child but having visited her mother decided not to do so. The plaintiff signed the form consenting to placement for adoption on 27 May 1979. This document was explained to her by a representative of the third named defendant society. She subsequently informed the society that she wanted the child placed. The plaintiff's husband was opposed to the adoption, and subsequently the plaintiff refused her consent and went to America with her husband indicating that she would like the child to be put in a home. No vacancy could be found in any such home, and the plaintiff subsequently wrote indicating that she wished to keep the child but without indicating what she proposed to do with him. The plaintiff returned to Ireland in January 1981 but took no step to recover the infant until she issued proceedings for sole custody in April 1981. The adoptive parents issued proceedings in November 1980 for an order authorising the Adoption Board to dispense with the consent of the plaintiff to the infant's adoption. The evidence disclosed that the first and second named defendants were excellent parents and that the infant had become attached to them and to their other child. The plaintiff and her husband were in a position to make adequate provision for the infant.

Held The plaintiff knew exactly what she was doing when she signed the consent to placement on 27 May 1979, and having been made fully aware of the consequences of such consent what the plaintiff wanted to do was to have the child adopted. The fact that she might have made a different decision had she come from a differently oriented family, been wealthy or proposing to marry the father of the child did not alter this decision. (*G. v An Bord Uchtala, S v Eastern*

Health Board and Others applied). On the evidence the infant was particularly subject to stress upon removal from the family into which it had become integrated and it was in the best interest of the child to refuse the application by the plaintiff for custody.

Cases referred to in judgment
G v An Bord Uchtala [1980] IR 32
S v The Eastern Health Board, High Court (Finlay P) 28 February 1979
McC v An Bord Uchtala

Reported at [1983] ILRM 228

COMPANY

In the Matter of Clubman Shirts Ltd; And in the Matter of the Companies Acts, 1963 to 1977; And in the Matter of ss. 205 and 371 of the Companies Act, 1963: High Court 1981 No. 1825P (O'Hanlon J) 19 November 1982

Company - S.205 relief - Whether affairs of the company being exercised in an oppressive manner in respect of minority shareholder - Numerous breaches of statutory obligations as to meetings and accounts - Failure of directors to respond to requests for information - Company divesting itself of all its assets and liabilities - Whether minority shareholder dealt with fairly - Whether oppression made out - Companies Act 1963, *(No.* 33) *s.* 205

Facts The petitioner owned or controlled about 20 per cent of the equity in the company. He brought a petition under s. 205 of the Companies Act, 1963 alleging that the affairs of the company had been and were being carried on, and the powers of the directors had been and were being exercised, in a manner oppressive to him. The company had failed to hold annual general meetings or to present audited accounts or to file annual returns in a number of years. The directors refused to give the petitioner information to which he was entitled under the Companies Acts. The directors offered to buy the petitioner's shares at a low figure and the petitioner alleged that this involved unfair pressure as the directors had not given him the information which they possessed and which was necessary to assess the value of the shares. In 1980, when the company was in grave financial difficulties and threatened with receivership and probably liquidation, the directors transferred the entire business undertaking and the assets of the company to another company in a deal which extricated the company from its financial liabilities but which did not involve any payment to shareholders. The petitioner was not given full details of this transaction at the time. The petitioner alleged that all this constituted oppression.

Held The failures in relation to annual meetings, accounts, annual returns and the giving of information were examples of negligence, carelessness and irregularity, but were not part of a deliberate scheme to deprive the petitioner of his rights or to cause him loss or damage and did not constitute oppression. In relation to the offers to buy the petitioner's shares the directors were entitled to offer any price with any conditions. As the petitioner on receipt of these offers had never said that he was unable to assess the value of his shares due to lack of information, and had never requested any information for such purpose, and as he had never sold or considered selling any of his shares no claim for relief under s. 205 could succeed. The transfer in 1980 was a bona fide agreement made on the well-founded belief that it was the only way to avoid receivership and probable liquidation. The failure to give the petitioner full information about this transfer gave him genuine ground for complaint, but there were reservations about putting it into the category of oppressive conduct. An order would be made directing the majority shareholders to buy the plaintiff's shares based on their true value as of 31 July 1980 which was the date when he should have been given a fuller opportunity of concurring or not concurring in the transfer embarked on by the majority shareholders.

No cases referred to in judgment

[This case is under appeal]

Reported at [1983] ILRM 323

The Revenue Commissioners v John Donnelly: Supreme Court 1981 No. 164 (O'Higgins CJ, Henchy and Hederman JJ) *Nem Diss.* 24 February 1983.

Company - Liquidation - Sale of properties - Liability incurred for corporation tax - Whether such tax an expense incurred in the realisation of an asset - Whether such tax a necessary disbursement of the liquidator - Companies Act, 1963, (No. 33) s. 285(2)(ii) - Winding up Rules O 77 r. 129

Revenue - Company liquidation - Sale of properties - Liability incurred for corporation tax - Whether such tax an expense incurred in the realisation of an asset - Whether such tax a necessary disbursement of the liquidator - Companies Act 1963, s. 285(2)(ii) - Winding Up Rules O 77 r.129 - Capital Gains Tax Act, 1975 (No. 20)

Facts The respondent, as liquidator of Van Hool McArdle Ltd, sold certain property which incurred a liability for corporation tax on chargeable gains accrued on the sale under the Capital Gains Tax Act, 1975. The respondent brought a motion in the High Court seeking certain directions which included:
1. Whether or not capital gains tax was payable in relation to the sale of an 'expense' incurred in the realisation of an asset within the meaning of O. 77 r. 129 of the Rules of the Superior Courts, which relate to winding up.
2. If it is payable, can it be deducted from the proceeds of sale payable to the mortgagee?

3. Is the tax 'a necessary disbursement' of the liquidator under the third heading listed in r. 129?

In the High Court, Carroll J answered separately in the negative to all three questions. The appellants appealed against the reply to the third question only. In ruling on the third question Carroll J expressed the opinion that the corporation tax did not qualify for priority payment under section 285(2)(ii) of the Companies Act, 1963 as the tax had not been assessed within the time stipulated by the statute.

Held (O'Higgins CJ, Henchy and Hederman JJ concurring) In dismissing the appeal: r. 129 is intended to deal with costs and expenses, and does not include a liability of the company for corporation tax.

Case referred to in judgment
In the Matter of Van Hool McArdle Ltd (in liquidation) And In the Matter of The Companies Act, 1963 [1982] ILRM 340

Reported at [1983] ILRM 329

Continental Irish Meat Ltd (in Receivership and in Voluntary Liquidation) v The Minister for Agriculture: High Court 1982 No. 1207 (McMahon J) 7 March 1983.

European Economic Community - Company liquidation - Company owning a sum for monetary compensation levies - Company owned a sum for monetary compensation payments on farm levies - Intervention agent claiming a right of set-off - Whether claims exist in the same right - Whether intervention agent acting as agent for the importing State - EEC Council Regulation 25/62- EEC Council Regulation 729/70, articles 2, 3, 4 - EEC Council Regulation 974/71, article 2 (a).

Facts From January 1977 to July 1977 the plaintiff company exported meats from Ireland to the United Kingdom and Italy. The plaintiff went into liquidation in 1977 owing the defendant a sum for monetary compensation levies for meat exports from Ireland but was entitled to receive from the defendant a larger sum as monetary compensation payments on imports of meat into the United Kingdom from Italy. The defendant claimed a right of set off in respect of a sum of equal amount consisting of levies admittedly due by the plaintiff to the defendant as intervention agent in respect of farm produce exported from Ireland.

Held by MacMahon J in finding for the plaintiff:
(i) The right of set-off being a matter of procedure must be determined by the *lex fori* and therefore the defendant cannot maintain the set-off claimed unless the claims exist between the parties in the same right.

(ii) The defendant in paying monetary compansation amounts which should be granted by the importing member state is doing so as agent for the importing state and on its behalf. Therefore he is not acting in the same capacity when as intervention agent carrying out the common agricultural policy on behalf of the state he charges monetary compensation amounts on exports.

Cases referred to in judgment
Pesch's Case (1973) ECR 2705

Reported at [1983] ILRM 503

In The Matter of Pageboy Couriers Ltd and In The Matter of The Companies Act 1963-1982: High Court 1983 No. 1565P (O'Hanlon J) 27 April 1983

Company - Creditor seeking order for the compulsory winding up of a company - Claim that company indebted to petitioning creditor - Company disputing petitioner's entitlement - whether winding up proceedings should be brought where petitioner is aware that company has a substantial and reasonable defence.

Facts The petitioner commenced proceedings by summary summons against Pageboy Couriers Ltd (the 'company') in which he claimed payment of the sum of £5,000 due in respect of 2 years' directors fees. The company issued a notice for particulars to the petitioner as plaintiff in the summary matter requesting particulars of the agreement under which it was alleged that the plaintiff was entitled to such fees. In reply to the notice for particulars the plaintiff his claim arose from an agreement made between himself and a director of the company. The plaintiff then allowed his civil proceedings to lie dormant after receiving the notice for particulars and did not prosecute them at any further stage. Instead, he brought a petition to wind up the company in reliance upon the same claim which was at all times disputed by the company on the grounds that the agreement had not secured the sanction of the company.

Held by O'Hanlon J: As the petitioner's claim had at all times been disputed by the company in good faith and on substantial grounds the petition would be dismissed.

Cases referred to in judgment
Mann v Goldstein [1968] 1 WLR 1091 [1968] 2 All ER 769
Stonegate Securities Ltd v Gregory [1980] 3 WLR 168 : [1980] 1 All ER 241, CA

Cases cited in legal argument
Re Gold Hill Mines (1882) 23 Ch D 210
Stonegate Securities Ltd v Gregory (*Supra*)

Reported at [1983] ILRM 510

Patrick McGowan, Thomas Robinson, Barbara McGovern, Andrew Gillespie and Albert Bartlet and (by order) Food Products (Donegal) Ltd v Joseph Gannon: High Court 1982 No. 11751P (Carroll J) 25 January 1983

Company Law - Company in receivership - Guarantor and sundry creditors seeking information concerning the proposed purchase price of the assets - Whether guarantor entitled to the information - Whether sale be restrained.
Tort - Negligence - Duty of care - Company in receivership - Whether receiver owes duty of care to guarantor.

Facts A guarantor and certain creditors (the first five named plaintiffs) of a company (the sixth named plaintiff) sought to restrain the sale of the company's factory premises by a receiver (the defendant) appointed under a debenture as agent of the company, on the apprehension that it was being sold at less than full value. Initially, neither the guarantor nor the creditors (some of whom were also directors of the company) knew any of the details of the proposed sale. They then applied as a preliminary issue of the injunction proceedings at the hearing to restrain the sale until they were informed of the sale price, and for time to consider their position in the light of that information. The matter was adjourned for a week to enable the plaintiffs to ascertain if the company required the information and wished to be joined as a plaintiff. The directors resolved that the company be joined, and they then sought the information regarding the sale. This was supplied by the defendant to the company in confidence. The issue at the resumed hearing was whether the guarantor and creditors individually were entitled to that information as of right. A further question for determination was whether the company could restrain the defendant from the proposed sale at an undervalue; or having found the market demand to be inadequate, should wait for any given period in the hope of a better price.

Held 1. The receiver owes a duty of care to the guarantor of a company, but, unlike the position of a potential beneficiary under a discretionary trust, the receiver is not a trustee for the guarantor nor is there any contractual relationship between them. The creditors were in no better position. Therefore, neither the guarantor nor creditors as such were entitled to the information sought.
2. It was clear that following decided cases the company is concerned that no contract be signed if there is danger of sale at an undervalue. The receiver owes a duty to the company to use reasonable care to obtain the best price available.
3. In all the circumstances, including the divergence of valuations of the premises on both sides, the sale should be restrained for a further 3 weeks so that the company might consider its position in the light of the information which it had just received.

Cases referred to in judgment
Casey v Irish Intercontinental Bank [1979] IR 364
Chaine-Nickson v The Bank of Ireland & Ors [1976] IR 393
Standard Chartered Bank Ltd v Walker & Anor [1982] 3 All ER 938

Reported at [1983] ILRM 516

Christopher Gunning v The Right Honourable The Lord Mayor and Burgesses of Dublin: High Court 1981 No. 96SS (Carroll J) 24 June 1982.

Compulsory Purchase - Compensation - Realignment of road necessitating acquisition of motor repair business - Claimant, in order to mitigate loss, acquiring alternative premises prior to the service of notice - Whether acquiring authority liable to compensate claimant for losses occasioned before service - Assessment of compensation for disturbance - Whether identical with damages for breach of contract or for tort - Acquisition of Land (Assessment of Compensation) Act 1919, (Ch. 57) s. 2 rr 2, 6 - Housing Act 1969, (No. 16) s. 84.

Facts The applicant owned property in respect of which a compulsory purchase order was made by the respondent on 18 November 1976. A notice to treat dated 7 September 1978 was served on the applicant followed by a notice to enter dated the 19 September 1978. Having inspected the relevant map in the respondent's office in January 1974 confirming that a proposed road realignment would necessitate the acquisition of his premises and motor car repair business, the applicant decided that it was essential in order to mitigate his loss to acquire alternative premises and to have them equipped before the respondents took possession. Such premises were acquired and the applicant went into possession in March 1978. In addition to the market value of his premises at the date of the service of the notice to treat, the applicant also sought compensation for relocation costs, temporary loss of business, double overheads, loss of time in seeking new premsies, and miscellaneous disturbance. The respondents submitted that they were not liable for losses occasioned before the service of the notice to treat, or for double overheads from the date of notice to treat to the date on which possession was taken by the respondents since such losses arose from the fact that the applicant had relocated his business prior to the service of the notice to treat.

Held The underlying principle was the principle of equivalence, and the owner should be able to recover personal loss imposed by the forced sale and should recover neither more nor less than his total loss. Where the value of the land is to be ascertained on the date of service of the notice to treat, the element of compensation for disturbances is not ascertained by reference to estimated losses on that date but is ascertained when the award is made by reference to actual losses already incurred, with estimated future losses where relevant. Accordingly, if an arbitrator can hold (1) the steps taken in mitigation are clearly referable to an anticipated notice to treat, (2) that it is possible to show that an inevitable loss consequent on the notice to treat has been avoided, and (3) that the steps taken, while not obligatory, were reasonable and prudent and had not been taken for a collateral purpose, then the arbitrator might properly award those expenses and losses incurred, provided the costs of the steps taken in mitigation of losses resulting from those steps did not exceed the amount which could be awarded if no steps could have been taken until after the service of the notice to treat. Double overheads could be claimed only in so far as they were reasonable.

Cases referred to in judgment
Bloom (Kosher) & Sons Ltd v Tower Hamlets London Borough Council (1978) 35 P & C R 423; (1977) 247 EG 1091
Harvey v Crawley Development Corporation [1957] 1 QB 485
Horn v Sutherland Corporation [1941] 2 KB 26
Hunter v Manchester City Council [1975] 1 QB 877
Richet v Metropolitan Railway Co. (1867) LR 2 HL 175 HL(E)
West Midland Baptist (Trust) Assoc. Inc. v Birmingham Corporation [1970] AC 874; [1969] 3 WLR 389

Reported at [1983] ILRM 56

CONSTITUTION

The State (Rohan Whelan) v The Governor of Mountjoy Prison: High Court 1981 No. 333SS (Barrington J) 21 December 1981.

Constitution - Arrest and detention under emergency powers legislation - Conviction - Application for habeas corpus - Allegation that prosecutor had not been charged with the offences of which he was convicted - Principal authority on which prosecutor relied in the course of being reviewed by the Supreme Court - Matter adjourned by consent to the next list and prosecutor admitted to bail - On whether such procedure unconstitutional - whether an adjournment upon a return date warranted under the provision of Article 40 - Constitituon of Ireland 1937, Article 40.4

Facts The prosecutor was arrested under s. 2 of the Emergency Powers Act, 1976. He applied for habeas corpus on the ground that he had not been charged, before a court, with the offences of which he was subsequently convicted. A conditional order was granted and the case came on for hearing on 11 January 1979. The prosecutor was relying on a High Court decision which at that time was under review by the Supreme Court. Pending the Supreme Court's decision the matter was adjourned by consent. The implication of the Supreme Courts' decision, overruling the High Court, was that the original detention of the prosecutor had been in accordance with law. The prosecutor now brought a fresh application for an absolute order of habeas corpus on the grounds that the procedure adopted by the High Court on 11 January 1979 in failing to discharge the conditional order and adjourning the hearing had been unconstitutional.

Held Although Art. 40.4.2° imposes a duty on the High Court to enquire 'forthwith' into the lawfulness of a person's detention, the court, while appreciating the urgent nature of such an application, must interpret the section as it thinks best in the interests of justice and, notwithstanding the provisions of Art 40.4.3° there was nothing in the Constitution which demanded that proceedings of this nature be completed on the day named for the hearing. Accordingly the prosecutor's detention was in accordance with the law as laid down by the Supreme Court in *The State (Walsh) v Maguire*, overruling *The State (Brennan) v Mahon* upon which the prosecutor had relied. Application dismissed.

Cases referred to in judgment
State (Brennan) v Mahon High Court 1975 No. 288SS (Finlay P) 13 February 1978
State (Walsh) v Maguire [1979] IR 372
State (Burke) v Lennon [1940] IR 136
State (Browne) v Feran [1967] IR 147

Reported at [1983] ILRM 52

James P. McCann, v The Attorney General and The Racing Board:
High Court 1977 No. 6281P (Barron J) 28 July 1982

Constitution - Licensed bookmaker - Revocation of course betting permit - Whether invalid - Whether Racing Board administering justice - Entitlement to fair procedures - Whether hearing contrary to natural justice - Locus standi - Constitution of Ireland 1937, Articles 37, 40.3 - Racing Board and Racecourses Act, 1945 (No. 16) s. 24.

Facts The plaintiff granted course betting permit by the Board on 25 April 1968 and thereafter the plaintiff carried on business as bookmaker at race meetings throughout the country. He also opened a betting shop and was bookmaker at several greyhound racing meetings. On 24 November 1973, Board officials complained that plaintiff's clerk entered two bets on his own racing card instead of the standard racing sheet at Navan. Plaintiff's solicitors wrote to the Board pointing out that transactions complained of were carried out by the clerk and not by the plaintiff. The plaintiff's betting permit was revoked by the Board on 18 December 1973. He appealed and the appeal was heard by the Board on 21 December 1973. When revocation was confirmed, the plaintiff brought these proceedings claiming that s. 24 of the Racing Board and Racecourses Act 1945 was unconstitutional by purporting to give the Board power to administer justice in a criminal matter; that the Board was given power to administer justice in which its powers were not limited; that the Board was given unfettered discretion; that the plaintiff was denied a hearing before the revocation; and that the hearing of the appeal was not in accordance with natural justice as it was heard by the same body which had originally revoked the permit.

Held 1. That the powers granted to the Board are not such as are reserved to judges as being properly regarded as the administration of justice. 2. Even though the Board could make its decision to revoke without a hearing, this of itself was not a denial of fair procedures as an appeal — requiring a hearing — was provided for in the statute. 3. The hearing of an appeal by the same body which heard the original complaint is not a denial of fair procedures.

Cases referred to in judgment
In re Solicitors Act, 1954 No. 36 [1960] IR 239
McDonald v Bord na gCon [1965] IR 217
Cahill v Sutton [1980] IR 269
East Donegal Co-Operative Society Ltd. v Attorney-General [1970] IR 317
State (Duffy) v Minister for Defence SC No. 17/1979 9 May 1979
O'Donoghue v Veterinary Council [1975] IR 398

Reported at [1983] ILRM 67

Vincent O'Sullivan v Sean Hartnett, The Attorney General and Ireland: Supreme Court 1981 No. 14 (O'Higgins CJ, Henchy and Griffin JJ) 26 October 1982 (Nem. Diss).

Constitution - Criminal Law - Unlawful possession of salmon - Summary conviction - Fine and confiscation of catch - Whether minor offence - Whether need to review the criteria laid down in the decided cases - Petty Sessions (Ireland) Act, 1851 (Ch. 93) s. 22 - Fisheries (Consolidation) Act, 1959, (No. 14) ss 182(2)(a), 182(4).

Facts The plaintiff had been charged in the District Court with two offences concerning the unlawful capture of 900 salmon contrary to s. 182(2)(a) of the Fisheries (Consolidation) Act, 1959. S. 182(4) in providing for a penalty on summary conviction necessarily implies that the case be tried summarily. Before the hearing of the charge the plaintiff sought a declaration in the High Court that the offences could not be said to be minor offences, and consequently that s. 182(4) was unconstitutional having regard to Art. 38.5 which requires that non-minor offences be tried with a jury. McWilliam J held that the offences charged were not minor. The order of the High Court declared that 'offences under s. 182(2)(a) of the Fisheries (Consolidation) Act, 1959 are not minor offences'. The defendants appealed against this order.

Held The judgment of McWilliam J showed that he had decided no more than that the particular offences charged in this instance are not minor offences. He did not go so far as to say that all offences under the section are non-minor offences. It is a matter of construction in cases such as the present one, where the penalty depends on the particular circumstances, whether the offence is minor or not. If this plaintiff were to be found guilty he would be liable to pay a fine of almost £10,000, or to six months imprisonment, as well as to forfeiture of the 900 salmon. Therefore, the severity of the consequences of conviction in the circumstances of the case marks the particular offences charged as being other than minor. Appeal allowed only to the extent of varying the declaration of the High Court to be that neither of the particular offences charged against the plaintiff is a minor offence.

Case referred to in judgment
Vincent O'Sullivan v Sean Hartnett, AG and Ireland [1981] ILRM 469

Reported at [1983] ILRM 79

The State (Sean Lynch) v Patrick Cooney, Minister for Posts and Telegraphs and the Attorney General of Ireland: Supreme Court 1982 No. 44 (O'Higgins CJ, Walsh J, Henchy J, Griffin and Hederman JJ) 28 July 1982

Broadcasting Authority - Constitution - Judicial review - Order preventing access by Provisional Sinn Fein candidates to radio and television to promote their electoral campaign - Whether violation of the provisions of the Constitution - Whether Minister's opinion that the broadcasting would be likely to promote, or incite to crime, etcetera, reviewable by the courts - Locus standi - Whether certiorari an appropriate procedure for challenging the validity of legislation - Constitution of Ireland 1937, Article 40.6.1° - Broadcasting Authority Act 1960 (No. 10), s. 31(1) - Broadcasting Authority (Amendment) Act 1976 (No. 37), s.16.

Facts The prosecutor (Sean Lynch) was one of seven Sinn Fein candidates in the General Election of February 1982. To qualify for broadcasting time on Radio Telefis Eireann (hereinafter RTE) it was necessary for a political party to have seven or more candidates in the field. As Sinn Fein had the requisite number of candidates RTE agreed to allocate time to that party for a series of party political broadcasts. The prosecutor was selected by Sinn Fein to make the broadcast on its behalf. The first defendant, Patrick Cooney acting as as Minister for Posts and Telegraphs made an order in exercise of the powers conferred on him by the Broadcasting Authority Act 1960 s. 31 (No. 2) Order, 1982. (SI 21 of 1982) which directed RTE to refrain from broadcasting any matter made by or on behalf or advocating, offering or inviting support for the organisation styling itself Provisional Sinn Fein. The amended sub-section reads:

> (i) Where the Minister is of the opinion that the broadcasting of a particular matter or any matter of a particular class would be likely to promote, or incite to crime or would tend to undermine the authority of the State, he may by order direct the authority to refrain from broadcasting the matter or any matter of the particular class, and the authority shall comply with the order.
>
> (1)(a) An order under sub-s. (1) of this section shall remain in force for a period not

exceeding 12 months as is specified in the order and the period for which the order is to remain in force and may be extended or further extended by an order made by the Minister or by a resolution passed by both Houses of the Oireachtas providing for its extension; provided that the period for which an order under the said sub-s. (1) is extended or further extended by an order or resolution under this sub-section shall not exceed a period of 12 months.

(1)(b) Every order made by the Minister under this section shall be laid before each House of the Oireachtas as soon as may be after it is made and, if a resolution annulling the order is passed by either such House within the next 21 days on which that House has sat after the order is laid before it the order shall be annulled accordingly but without prejudice to its validity prior to the annullment.

The prosecutor challenged the validity of the amending of the amended sub-section on the general grounds that it constituted an infringement of the citizen's right freely to express convictions and opinions as provided for in Article 40.6.1° of the Constitution, and that *inter alia* the Minister's opinion expressed in the order which he makes is not reviewable by the courts and that the Minister is given an absolute and unfettered discretion to act as he thinks fit.

It was held in the High Court by O'Hanlon J that the inclusion of the words "is of opinion" as expressed in the section, does not permit of a judicial review of the opinion formed by the Minister, so as to determine whether it is legally valid or not. In appealing the High Court order of certiorari the respondents contended that the prosecutor did not have sufficient *locus standi* to make the application.

Held by the Supreme Court in allowing the appeal, (1) that s. 31(1) of the Broadcasting Authority Act 1960, as amended, does not confer on the Minister, the wide unfettered and sweeping powers alleged by the prosecutor; (2) When a statute confers a decision making power affecting personal rights on a non judicial person or body, conditional on that person or body reaching a prescribed opinion or conclusion based on a subjective assessment, a person who shows that a personal right of his has been breached by a decision purported to have been made in the exercise of that power has standing to seek, and the High Court jurisdiction to give, a ruling as to whether the pre-condition for the valid exercise of the power has been complied with in a manner that is *inter vires* the statute; (3) When the Oireachtas conferred the powers on the Minister to invoke s. 31 it intended that they be exercised only in conformity with the Constitution; (4) The prosecutor did have *locus standi* to maintain proceedings. The applicant was deprived by ministerial order of a benefit lawfully accorded to him and he was therefore entitled to complain if the deprivation was unlawful. *Cahill v Sutton* [1980] IR 269 applied.

Cases referred to in judgment
In re Art. 26 of the Constitution and the Offences Against the State Act, The State (Amendment) Bill 1940, [1940] IR 470.
Attorney General v Ryan's Car Hire Ltd [1965] IR 642
State (Burke) v Lennon [1940] IR 136.
Cahill v Sutton [1980] IR 269
East Donegal Co-Operative v AG [1970] IR 317

The Inland Revenue Commissioners v National Federation of Self-Employed and Small Businesses Ltd. [1981] 2 All ER 93
Loftus v Attorney General and Others [1979] IR 221
Mogul of Ireland v Tipperary (NI) Co. Co. [1976] IR 260
McDonald v Bord na gCon [1964] IR 350
State (Nicolaou) v An Bord Uchtala [1966] IR 567
In re O'Laighleis [1960] IR 93
Regina (Bridgman) v Drury [1894] 2 IR 489
Regina v The Greater London Council, Ex Parte Blackburn [1976] 3 All ER 184
The Transport Salaried Staff's Assoc. v CIE [1965] IR 180

Reported at [1983] ILRM 89

Re Reference Under Article 26 of the Constitution of the Housing (Private Rented Dwellings) Bill 1981: Supreme Court 1981 No. 341 (O'Higgins CJ, Walsh J, Henchy J, Griffin and Hederman JJ) 19 February 1982.

Constitution - Article 26 reference - Landlord and Tenant - Bill affecting rent and security of tenure - Landlords receiving an amount of rent substantially less than the market rent - Whether unjust attack on their property rights - Housing (Private Rented Dwellings) Bill 1981, Constitution of Ireland 1937, Articles 26, 40.3.2°

Facts On 24 December 1981 under Art. 26.1 of the Constitution, the President referred the Housing (Private Rented Dwellings) Bill 1981 for consideration by the Supreme Court. The Bill was intended to deal with the situation resulting from the court's declaration of the unconstitutionality of the Rent Restrictions Act 1960-67 (cf *Blake & Others v AG and Madigan v AG* [1981] ILRM 34) and was intended to apply to all formerly controlled dwellings. The long title to the Bill described it as intended *inter alia* 'to provide in accordance with the exigencies of the common good for a measure of security of tenure for the tenants of certain dwellings, for a reasonable return for landlords ... and for the eventual cesser of the entitlement of such tenants to retain possession of such dwellings ...' The Bill provided that a tenant should have a statutory entitlement to retain possession of the said dwelling during his lifetime, the lifetime of his spouse and thereafter in respect of a qualified member of his family for a period of 20 years from the commencement of the act. Under s. 6 the District Court was obliged to determine in default of agreement the gross rent of such dwellings on the basis of what a willing lessee not in occupation would give and a willing lessor take as reduced by an allowance for improvements, the said rent to be reviewed after five years. S. 9 provided that in respect of the years 1982 to 1986 the actual rent to be paid by a tenant was to be the rent payable at the commencement of the Act plus 40% of the difference between that rent and the rent fixed by the court in 1982, in 1983 55% of that difference, in 1984 70% of that difference, in 1985, 85% of that difference and in 1986 and thereafter the rent fixed by the court.

Held (O'Higgins CJ delivering the Judgment of the Court) The effect of the rebates was that for a period of five years after the passing of the Bill, landlords were to receive an amount which would be substantially less than the just and proper rent payable in respect of their property and in the absence of any constitutionally permitted justification, this clearly constituted an unjust attack upon their property rights and was accordingly in contravention of the provisions of Art 40.3.2° of the Constitution.

Cases referred to in judgment
Blake and Others v Attorney General and *Madigan v Attorney General* [1981] ILRM 34
Ryan v Attorney General [1965] IR 294

Reported at [1983] ILRM 246

Richard O'Brien v Bord na Mona and the Attorney General: Supreme Court 1981 No's 201 & 205 (O'Higgins CJ, Finlay P, Walsh, Henchy and Griffin JJ) 9 December 1982 (Nem diss. on non-Constitutional matter).

Constitution - Bord na Mona - Power to compulsorily acquire bogland - Whether power of judicial nature - Absence of right of appeal - Whether statutory provisions invalid - Whether procedures adopted in breach of natural justice - Distinction between procedures in relation to the decision to acquire and procedures in relation to the assessment of fair compensation - Constitution of Ireland 1937, Articles 40.3, 43 - Turf Development Act 1946 (No. 10), ss. 17, 28, 30-36.

Facts S. 29 of the Turf Development Act, 1946 provides that Bord na Mona, the first defendant may for the purpose of exercising its functions compulsorily acquire various rights in or over land. S. 30 provides that the Bord may, subject to provisions for payment of compensation and the giving of due notice, take possession of any land, or exercise any right in land, or terminate, restrict or interfere with interest in such land. The plaintiff is the owner of a farm in County Westmeath which includes an area of bog land. The defendants published an advertisement in local newspapers indicating their intention to acquire certain land including 132 acres of the plaintiff's bog land. The plaintiff objected to the Bord and made certain other submissions with a group of local farmers. However, while the objections to the acquisitions were communicated to representatives of the first defendant only some of the complaints were brought to the attention of the defendant's board of directors who acceded to the recommendations that the plaintiff's land should be compulsorily acquired. The plaintiff sought a declaration (i) that s. 29 and s. 30 of the Act were repugnant to Articles 40 and 43 of the Constitution as they failed to respect, defend and vindicate the personal rights of the plaintiff as guaranteed by Article 40. s. 3, and that they contravene the plaintiff's right to private ownership of his lands guaranteed in Article 43; (ii) in the alternative that Bord na Mona acted *ultra* *vires* their powers and in breach of the rules of natural and constitutional justice.

In the High Court it was held by Keane J, that the compulsory purchase of the plaintiff's lands was a judicial and not an administrative act, and the power contained in the Act enabling the defendants to act without a form of appeal or confirmation by an external tribunal violated the maxim of natural justice and of constitutional justice.

Held by the Court:
(i) in allowing the appeal setting aside the judgment of the High Court that s. 29 and s. 30 of the Turf Development Act, 1946 are not invalid having regard to the provisions of the Constitution;
(ii) The first defendant was acting in an administrative capacity subject to the restrictions imposed by the Constitution. Any arbitrary or capricious use of the powers designated by the Turf Development Act, 1946 is subject to the full rigour of judicial review.
(iii) *Per* **Finlay** P (O'Higgins CJ, Walsh, Henchy and Griffin JJ concurring) the failure of the first defendants properly to hear the plaintiff's representations and objections was a breach of the necessity for the observance of certain procedure and natural justice.

Cases referred to in judgment
East Donegal CoOperative v the Attorney General [1970] IR 317
Fisher v The Irish Land Commission & the Attorney General [1948] IR 3
Loftus v the Attorney General [1979] IR 221
McDonald v Bord na gCon & the Attorney General [1965] IR 217
Murphy v Dublin Corporation [1972] IR 215

Reported at [1983] ILRM 314

James G. O'Callaghan v The Commissioners of Public Works in Ireland, Ireland and the Attorney General: High Court 1979 No. 5892P (McWilliam J) 4 October 1982

Constitution - National Monument - Preservation order - Effect of order - Whether unjust attack on property rights - Whether 'monuments' confined to things specifically mentioned in s. 2 - Whether order made in conformity with principles of natural justice - National Monuments Act 1930 (No. 2) ss. 2, 8, 11 - National Monuments (Amendment) Act 1954 (No. 37) s. 3 - Constitution of Ireland, 1937, Articles 40, 43.

Facts On 1 March 1977 the plaintiff contracted to purchase a 46 acre farm for £115,000. About 38 or 39 acres of the farm comprise a promontory fort known as Loughshinney Promontory Fort. The farm had been used solely for grazing for a very long time. The plaintiff purchased the farm to set his son up with an equestrian centre and to enable him to engage in horticulture. The Commissioners in exercise of powers conferred by s. 8 of the 1954 Act, had served a notice dated 26 April 1970 on the plaintiff's immediate predecessor in title of their intent to list the promontory in *Iris Oifigiuil* as a monument the preservation of which is of national importance. The monument was then so listed. The notice warned that the owner could not alter the monument in any way or make excavations nearby without either two months notice to the Commissioners or in case of urgency their consent. The plaintiff was verbally informed of the notice by the vendor and alleged that the vendor told him that it related to only part of the promontory.

The plaintiff commenced ploughing shortly after the contract and this disturbed items of archaeological interest. As a result, the Commissioners, acting under s. 8 of the 1930 Act as amended by s. 3 of the 1954 Act made a preservation order relating to the promontory. This prohibited any person from interfering with the monument in any way and from ploughing or disturbing the ground within or near the monument. The Commissioners have the power to revoke such orders. S. 8 does not provide for compensation. The preservation order was served on the contractor employed by the plaintiff and on 13 May 1977 after difficulty in locating the plaintiff, a letter was sent to him notifying him of the order. The plaintiff's solicitors unsuccessfully appealed against the order to the Office of Public Works. In June 1977 the plaintiff harrowed the ploughed ground scattering archaeological deposits.

The plaintiff brought this action seeking a declaration that s. 8 of the 1930 Act as amended by the 1954 Act is inconsistent with the Constitution and that, irrespective of whether that section was constitutional or not, the preservation order was of no effect due to breach of the requirements of national justice.

The plaintiff made three submissions.

1. That the 'sterilisation' of the lands without compensation was an unjust attack on the right to ownership and use of property guaranteed by Articles 40 and 43 of the Constitution.

2. That the provisons of the Acts enabling the Commissioners to 'sterilise' the land without a hearing either in the first instance or by way of appeal also offend against the Constitution as an unjust attack on the right to ownership and use of private property.

3. Even if the statutory provisions were constitutional, the preservation order was void because the procedures actually adopted were contrary to the principles of natural justice and in particular to the principle of *audi alteram partem*.

Held All the bundle of rights constituting the plaintiff's ownership of the fort had not been abolished, therefore Article 43.1.2° of the Constitution had not been infringed. The 'sterilisation' consisted merely of preventing the use of the lands for other more profitable purposes. The Oireachtas is clearly entitled to decide that it is for the common good that national monuments should be preserved. The plaintiff's lands were not chosen arbitrarily and the preservation order was for the common good of all citizens and not a limited class of citizen. For these reasons while the making of preservation orders without compensation was an attack on property rights it was not an unjust attack, therefore the first submission failed.

In relation to the second submission, there is a difference between prescribing a procedure for the interference with property rights which offends against the concepts of natural justice and providing for an interference which leaves the procedures to be arranged by the body effecting the interference. The statutory provisions in this case came within the record of these categories. The landowner has a right to have an honest endeavour made by the Commissioners to exercise fairly a discretion.

The second and third submissions depended upon the proposition that the procedures infringed the principles of natural justice. It was argued that the infringement consisted of making the order without first giving the plaintiff an opportunity of stating his case and of delay in giving him notice of the order. These submissions failed because the plaintiff knew of the notice of April 1970 and should have had no misapprehension of its effect. The Commissioners had grounds for thinking that the plaintiff might have continued to plough the promontory even if he had been notified of their intention to make the order. Also, no adequate ground for opposing the order had been made because it was not denied that the fort was a monument and the allegation that it had already been damaged by earlier ploughing had not been proved. The plaintiff's claim failed on all grounds.

Cases referred to in judgment
Attorney General v Southern Industrial Trust & Simons (1960) 94 ILTR 61
Blake & Ors v The Attorney General [1981] ILRM 34
Central Dublin Development Assoc. v The Attorney General (1975) 109 ILTR 69
Fisher v The Irish Land Commission [1948] IR 3
Pigs Marketing Board v Donnelly (Dublin) Ltd [1939] IR 413
The State (Quinn) v Ryan [1965] IR 70
Tormey v The Commissioners of Public Works Supreme Court 21 December 1972.

Cases referred to in legal argument
Blake & Others v Attorney General [1981] ILRM 34
Buckley & Others v Attorney General [1950] IR 67
Central Dublin Development Association v Attorney General (1975) 109 ILTR 69
City of Euclid v Amber Realty Co. (1926) 272 US 365
Cityview Press Ltd. v An Comhairle Oiliuna [1980] IR 381
Cotter v Aherne & Others, High Court 1975 No. 3410 P (Finlay P) 25 February 1977
East Donegal Livestock Mart Ltd & Ors v Attorney General [1970] IR 317
Foley v Irish Land Commission [1952] IR 118
The State (Gleeson) v Minister for Defence [1976] IR 280
Glover v BLN Ltd & Others [1973] IR 388
Goldblatt v Town of Hempstead (1962) 369 US 590
Hadacheck v Sebastian (1915) US 394
In the Matter of Padraig Haughey [1971] IR 217
Loftus & Others v Attorney General [1979] IR 221
Martin v Dublin Corporation Supreme Court 1979 No 133 p, 12 February 1979
Meskell v Coras Iompair Eireann [1973] IR 121
Miller v Schoene (1928) 276 US 272
Moynihan v Greensmyth [1977] IR 55
Murphy v Attorney General Supreme Court 1979 No. 183 25 January 1980
Tormey v Commissioners of Public Works Supreme Court 28 May 1976; High Court 21 December 1968

Reported at [1983] ILRM 391   [This case is under appeal]

Mark Cooke (An Infant, Suing by his Father and Next Friend William Cooke) v Patrick Walsh: High Court 1981 No. 1666P (Hamilton J) 11 January 1983

Negligence - Road traffic accident - Personal injuries - Assessment of future economic loss - Acturial evidence - Notional investment of capital sum - Rate of interest - Trustee (Authorised Investments) Act, 1958 (No. 8), ss. 1, 2(1), 3(1) - Trustee (Authorised Investments) Order 1977, S.I. (No. 344) 1977 - (Trustee Authorised Investments) (No. 2) Order 1972.

Constitution - Health Service - Legislation empowering Minister to make regulations in respect of medical services - Regulations rendering victims of road traffic accidents ineligible for free medical services - Whether exclusive law making authority of the National Parliament eroded by such delegation of power - Whether Minister acted ultra vires - Whether regulations unconstitutional as being discriminatory - Whether Minister acted in accordance with the principles of natural justice - Constitution of Ireland 1937, Arts 15, 40.3 - Health Act, 1970 (No. 1), ss. 45, 46, 51, 52(1), 53, 56, 72 - Health Services Regulations 1971, S.I. No.   of 1971 Art 6(3) - Health Services (Limited Eligibility) Regulations 1979. S.I. No. of 1979.

Facts The plaintiff, an infant, suffered serious personal injuries following a road traffic accident. At the trial of the action it was stated that the infant plaintiff who was 9 years of age at the time of the accident, had sustained injuries of such severity that he would require constant medical supervision, care and attention for the rest of his life. It was also accepted that his life span would not exceed a further 40 years. At the conclusion of the evidence relating to the circumstances of the accident and of the nature of the plaintiff's injuries it was agreed between the parties that the remaining issues should be determined by the trial judge sitting without a jury.

The trial judge (Hamilton J) found for the plaintiff on the basis of an apportionment of 80% on the defendant and 20% on the infant plaintiff. As the infant plaintiff would require constant care he would have to be taken into wardship. This would require the High Court to determine the mode of investment of the plaintiff's damages in accordance with its statutory obligations pursuant to s. 3(1) of the Trustee (Authorised Investments) Act, 1958 which limited the funds available for investment of the infant plaintiff's damages. Actuarial evidence was adduced on behalf of both parties to determine the present value of the infant plaintiff's future financial loss of earnings and the cost of future care. The cost of providing for the plaintiff for a period of 39 years was determined at £325 per week.

Actuarial evidence gave sets of figures allowing for devaluation. For the plaintiff it was submitted that the appropriate figure was that based on an interest rate of between 2% and 3%, and for the defendant it was suggested that the appropriate figure was based on an interest rate of 5%. The trial judge accepted the following actuarial evidence submitted on behalf of the plaintiff:

(i) that the average rate of inflation had been 14.5% per annum from 1970 to 1982; (ii) that the average annual return on investment in equities was less than that figure; (iii) that when the dividends were re-invested the real return on any of the permitted modes of investment was never more than 2% and often gave a negative return. The *principal* question to be determined was what was the rate of interest appropriate having regard to the permitted modes of investment, the rates of interest available and the current rate of inflation.

The plaintiff was a person with full eligibility for all the services to which an eligible person is entitled free of charges on payment under the provision of the Health Acts, particularly the Health Act, 1970. The plaintiff had been charged with such services on the grounds that he was rendered ineligible for free services by virtue of the provisions of the Health Services Regulations 1971 and more particularly Regulation 6(3) thereof. The effect of Article 6(3) of the Health Services (Limited Eligibility) Regulation, 1979 (SI) 110 of 1979 is to deprive a person, otherwise eligible, who requires treatment for injuries received in a road traffic accident, of services under ss. 52 and 56(2) of the Health Act, 1970, unless it is established to the satisfaction of the chief executive officer of the Health Board that he had not received or is entitled to receive damages or compensation in the nature of damages, from another person in respect of the injuries.

It was agreed by all parties to the proceedings that the provisions of sub-s. (3) excluded the plaintiff from what would have been free treatment for medical services pursuant to ss. 5 and 56(2) of the Health Act, 1970 since he was a person of full eligibility as defined in s. 45(1) of the Health Act, 1970. The power conferred on the Minister by s. 72(1) of the Health Act, 1970 is to make regulations to provide for any service under the Act being made available only to a particular class of persons who have eligibility for that service.

The issues raised by the defendants were as follows:
(i) Was s. 72 72(i) and (ii) of the Health Act, 1970 repugnant to the Constitution.
(ii) If the said s. 72(i) and (ii) of the Act was not repugnant to the Constitution was Article 6 (iii) of the Health Services Regulations 1971 (SI 105 of 1971) repugnant to the Constitution.
(iii) If neither such sub-sections of s. 72 nor Article 6 (iii) of the Health Services Regulations is repugnant to the Constitution was the Minister for Health acting ultra vires in making a law solely vested in the Oireachtas?
(iv) Did the defendant have any *locus standi* to raise the issues and to claim declarations in respect thereof?
There were, thus, two main issues for the court's determination and separate judgmentss were read in respect of each.

Held on the Damages Issue:

1. Hamilton J found that the plaintiff would suffer financial loss at the rate of £115 per week at present levels from the age of 18 to 51, and that the capital sum necessary to compensate for such financial loss could be determined by an actuary's calculation. Court practice has been to accept as relevant to the assessment of damages a valuation such that the capital sum awarded should represent the present value (as of the date of trial) of the loss of income and of

the future expenditure to be incurred as a result of the accident. The court must consider the amount of capital required to compensate the infant plaintiff at the rate of interest selected for valuation. In determining the rate of interest to be selected for valuation allowance must be made for devaluation in the value of money.

2. That for the purpose of investment of the capital sum awarded to the infant plaintiff the actuarial calculations should be based on a real interest yield of $2\frac{1}{2}\%$.

Held on the Constitutional Issue
(i) The provisions of s. 72(i) and (ii) of the Health Act, 1970 are not invalid having regard to the provisions of the Constitution.
(ii) Article 6(iii) of the Health Services Regulations 1971 (SI 105 of 71) is not repugnant to the Constitution.
(iii) The Minister for Health had acted *intra vires* in making the said regulation.
(iv) The obligation of the Minister in making a regulation operable under the Act is to act fairly and in accordance with the principles of Constitutional justice and the principle and policy of the Act.
(v) The defendant had the necessary *locus standi* to raise the foregoing issues in that he is liable to compensate the infant plaintiff for the loss sustained.

Cases referred to in judgment
NEGLIGENCE ISSUES:
Donnelly v Browne Supreme Court 1969 No. 153, 15 May 1982
Fletcher v Auto and Transporters Ltd [1968] 2 QB 322
Daniel Long v O'Brien and Cronin Ltd Supreme Court 1970 No. 107, 24 March 1972
McMorrow v Knott Supreme Court 1959 No 44, 21 December 1959
Paul and Another v Randall (1981) 55 ALJR 371
Swords v St Patrick's Copper Mines [1965] Ir Jur Rep 63

CONSTITUTIONAL ISSUES:
Cityview Press v An Chomhairle Oiliuna [1980] IR 381
East Donegal Cooperative v The Attorney General [1970] IR 317
McDonald v Bord na gCon [1965] IR 217

Diarmuid O'Donovan SC, Peter Sutherland SC and David Hamilton **for the plaintiff.**
T. K. Liston SC, Eoin Ryan SC and Frank Duggan **for the defendant**

Reported at [1983] ILRM 429   (Appeal allowed and retrial ordered.)

Michael Brennan, Dermot Clancy, Nicholas Fitzhenry, Bernard Devereux and Rory Brown v The Attorney General and Wexford County Council: High Court 1980 No. 10670 P (Barrington J) 23 July 1982.

Constitution - Pre-1937 statute of the UK parliament - Consistency - Valuation of agricultural land - Valuation carried out between 1852 and 1866 - No revaluation ever taking place - Valuation determining the extent of liability in respect of certain taxes, and the extent of eligibility for certain benefits - *Valuation unrelated to the circumstances of the present day - Whether an unjust attack on property rights - Whether arbitrary and unjust discrimination - Whether legislation, by virtue of its purported amendment in 1961, entitled to the benefit of the presumption of constitutionality - Constitution of Ireland 1937, Articles 40.1, 40.3 and 43 - Valuation (Ireland) Acts 1852 (Ch. 63) 1866 - Courts (Supplemental Provisions) Act, 1961. (No. 39).*

Facts The plaintiffs are members of an unincorporated association of Wexford farmers under the auspices of the Wexford branch of the Irish Farmers Association. As holders of agricultural land the valuation of such land is made by reference to an estimate of the net annual value thereof which in turn was estimated by reference to the average prices of certain agricultural products listed in s. 11 of the Valuation Act 1852 and which in turn represented an average of prices prevailing from 1849 to 1852. The valuation, known as 'The Griffith valuation' took a period of 14 years to complete for the whole of Ireland on a county by county basis from South to North. When the first valuation was conducted in 1852 agricultural holdings were depressed. Over the course of the following 14 years agriculture became more prosperous and rents rose, with the result that the valuation given to agricultural land in southern counties where the valuation had first been carried out were lower than those other counties where the work was conducted during more prosperous times. The amount of the rateable valuation (PLV) determined the extent of liability of farmers *inter alia* in payment of income tax and other revenue matters and the payment of rates on agricultural lands to the relevant county council. The plaintiffs claim:
(i) that the Valuation Acts constitute an invidious and unjust attack on property rights, contrary to Article 43 of the Constitution;
(ii) that the Act delimits the plaintiffs' rights of ownership in a manner inconsistent with the principles of social justice or in a manner not required by the exigencies of the common good;
(iii) the statutory provisions constitute an arbitrary and unjust discrimination against the plaintiffs, contrary to Article 40.1;
(iv) as a consequence, the rateable valuation of the plaintiffs' agricultural land is obsolete and contravenes the guarantee of basic fairness of procedures in legislation provided for in Article 40.3; failure to allow for any right of appeal against the valuation placed on their lands violates that guarantee;
(v) a declaration that the Valuation Acts 1852 to 1864, to the extent that they provide for the valuation for rating purposes of agricultural land within the State, are inconsistent with the Constitution.
The plaintiffs also submitted that because the Valuation Acts failed to provide a rational and fair system of valuing citizens' property they failed to hold the citizens equal before the law.

The defendants, while traversing the plaintiff's claim also pleaded:
(i) that the Oireachtas, from time to time, in the exercise of its constitutional obligation under, *inter alia* Articles 40 and 43 has provided appropriate relief

in respect of obligations imposed upon citizens upon the rateable valuation system; and

(ii) that the plaintiffs, not having exercised their rights under the provisions of the Valuations Acts with a view to bringing about an amendment of their valuation were not entitled to maintain these proceedings unless and until they had availed themselves of the said machinery.

The Attorney General submitted that the proper course for the plaintiffs to pursue was to bring a mandamus proceeding against Wexford County Council for an order directing the Council to apply to the Minister for Finance for a general revision of the valuation of the lands in County Wexford pursuant to s. 34 of the 1852 Act;

(b) that the Oireachtas by amending the Valuation Acts through the enactment of the Courts (Supplemental Provisions) Act, 1961, gave the Acts the status of post-constitutional Statutes, which were accordingly entitled to obtain the benefit of the presumption of constitutionality.

(c) that the taxation system and financial legislation generally were peculiarly matters for the Government and the Oireachtas, and that the management of the financial affairs of the State was given a peculiar status by the Constitution and was confirmed largely through the executive and the legislature.

Held (by Barrington J):

(i) That the property valuations made under the Valuation Acts on the plaintiffs' lands were not consistent with the Constitution, in that they did not respect the plaintiffs' property rights or respect the plaintiffs' rights to equality before the law in relation to their property rights.

(ii) The Valuation Acts were not carried forward by Article 50 of the Constitution, and they were not entitled to be regarded as post-constitutional Statutes by virtue of the Courts (Supplemental Provisions) Act 1961. The mere fact that a post-constitutional statute purports to amend or adopt a pre-constitutional statute does not extend the presumption of constitutionality to a pre-constitutional statute.

(iii) The plaintiffs' complaint was not an attack on financial legislation. It was merely directed against a unit of measure employed for valuation purposes, which was sufficient to maintain the plaintiffs in a situation of inequality.

(iv) That the form of appeal outlined in s. 34 of the 1852 Act was no longer applicable or practical in the circumstances. The plaintiffs were consequently denied a means of obtaining effective relief under existing law.

Cases referred to in judgment
In re Article 26 of the Constitution and *In the Matter of the Offences Against the State (Amendment) Bill,* [1940] IR 470
Blake & Others v The Attorney General [1981] ILRM 34
The State (Burke) v Lennon [1940] IR 136
Burke & Anor v Minister for Labour [1979] IR 354
Central Dublin Development Association v The Attorney General (1975) 109 ILTR 69
Charleston Association v Alderson 324 US 182
Dandridge v William 397 US 471
de Burca & Anor v The Attorney General [1976] IR 38
East Donegal Co-Operative Livestock Marts Ltd v The Attorney General [1970] IR 317

Foley v The Irish Land Commission [1952] IR 118
Gast Realty Co. v Schneider Granite Co. 240 US 55
Glover v BLN [1973] IR 388
Greene v Louisville and Interurban Railway Co. 244 US 499
The State (Hartley) v Governor of Mountjoy Prison Supreme Court 21 December 1967
In Re Haughey [1971] IR 217
Italy v The Commission [1963] ECR 165
Landers v Attorney General (1975) 109 ILTR 1
Lloyd Stores of Ohio v Bowers 358 US 522
McDonald v Bord na gCon [1965] IR 217
McGee v The Attorney General [1974] IR 284
McGowan v Maryland 366 US 420
McLaughlin v Florida 379 US 185
Melling v O Mathghamhna [1962] IR 1
Moynihan v Greensmyth [1977] IR 55
Murphy v The Attorney General Supreme Court 1979 No. 183 25 January 1980
Murtagh Properties v Cleary [1972] IR 330
Nebbia v New York 291 US 503
The State (Nicolaou) v An Bord Uchtala [1966] IR 567
O'Brien v Keogh [1972] IR 144
O'Brien v Manufacturing Engineering Co. [1973] IR 334
O'Byrne v The Minister for Finance [1959] IR 1
People (Attorney General) v Conmey [1975] IR 341
Royster Guano Co. v Virginia 253 US 412
The State (Quinn) v Ryan [1965] IR 70
Quinn's Supermarket v The Attorney General [1972] IR 1
Ryan v The Attorney General [1965] IR 294
San Antonio Independent School District v Rodriguez 411 US 1
The State (Sheerin) v Kennedy 1966 IR 379
Tax Commissioners v Jackson 283 US 522

Reported at [1983] ILRM 449　　　　　　　　　[This case is under appeal]

Donald Patrick Costello v The Director of Public Prosecutions and The Attorney General: High Court 1980 No. 4226P (Gannon J) 11 February 1983

Constitution - Criminal Law - Pre-trial procedures - District Justice deciding not to send accused for trial - Director of Public Prosecutions directing the accused be sent for trial by jury - Whether such power a judicial power - Constitution of Ireland 1937, Art. 34 - Courts of Justice Act 1936 (No. 48), s. 62 - Criminal Procedure Act 1967 (No. 12), ss. 5, 6, 7, 8 - Prosecution of Offences Act 1974 (No. 22), ss. 1, 2, 3 -

Facts The plaintiff was arrested under s. 30 of the Offences against the State Act, 1939, and was remanded in custody to appear before the District Court. The plaintiff appeared before the District Court on a number of occasions until his discharge by the district justice under s. 8 (5) of the Criminal Procedure Act, 1967. The first named defendant purported thereafter pursuant to s. 62 of the Courts of Justice Act, 1936 to direct that the plaintiff be sent forward for trial on the same charges upon which he had been discharged by the district justice. The plaintiff sought *inter alia* a declaration that s. 62 of the Courts of Justice Act 1936 was inconsistent with the Constitution, and that s. 3 of the Prosecution of Offences Act, 1974 which transferred to the first named defendant the functions and powers of the second named defendant under s. 62 of the 1936 Act was repugnant to the Constitution upon the grounds *inter alia*, firstly, that the function vested by s. 62 as amended by the 1967 and 1974 Acts was of such a judicial nature that it could only be exercised by the courts; and secondly that a direction under s. 62 amounted to a reversal of a judicial determination by the district court.

Held The function imposed on a district justice by the 1967 Act, while an investigative function to be exercised in a judicial manner, is not the determination of a justiciable controversy. It is rather a factor in the protection of the right to freedom of the individual, and the course which may be taken by an accused at such investigation does not alter the nature of this function of the District Justice. A direction under s. 62 of the 1936 Act is the initiation of a prosecution. It is not a judicial power or function nor does it require the exercise of a function or power of a judicial nature in a criminal matter such as is comprehended in Art. 37 of the Constitution. *The State (Shanahan) v AG* applied. Plaintiff's case dismissed.

Cases referred to in judgment
Buckley and others (Sinn Fein) v The Attorney General and Anor [1950] IR 67
Deaton v The Attorney General and The Revenue Commissioners [1963] IR 170
Lynam v Butler (No. 2) [1933] IR 74
The People (Attorney General) v Boggan [1958] IR 67
The State (C) v Minister for Justice and Ors [1967] IR 106
The State (Healy) v O'Donoghue and Ors [1976] IR 325
The State (O'Callaghan) v O'hUadhaigh [1977] IR 42
The State (Quinn) v Ryan and Ors. [1965] IR 70
The State (Shanahan) v The Attorney General and Ors. [1964] IR 239

[This case has been appealed to the Supreme Court: Judgment reserved]

Reported at [1983] ILRM 489

The People (Director of Public Prosecution) v Patrick Leo O'Shea: Supreme Court 1980 No. 190 (No. 1) (O'Higgins CJ, Finlay P, Walsh, Henchy and Hederman JJ) 2 November 1982

Constitution - Charge on indictment before Central Criminal Court - Jury, at the direction of the judge, recording verdict of not guilty - Whether open to Director of Public Prosecutions to bring an appeal against such verdict - Extent of Supreme Court's appellate jurisdiction - Plea of autrefois acquit explained - Constitution of Ireland 1937, Arts. 34.3.1°, 34.4.3°, 38.1, 38.5, 38.6 - Courts of Justice Act 1924

(*No.* 10) ss. 31, 63 - *Courts (Supplemental Provisions) Act* 1961 (*No.* 39), ss. 11(1), 48 - *Criminal Procedure Act* 1967 (*No.* 12), s. 34(1).

Facts Article 34.4.3° provides that 'the Supreme Court shall, with such exceptions and subject to such regulations as may be prescribed by law, have appellate jurisdiction from all decisions of the High Court, and shall also have appellate jurisdiction from such decisions of other courts as may be prescribed by law'. The respondent, Patrick Leo O'Shea was charged with certain offences before the Central Criminal Court. The trial commenced on 18 March 1980, and on 20 March 1980 the jury, by direction of the trial judge, found him not guilty of all charges and he was discharged from custody. An appeal was brought by the Director of Public Prosecutions against the trial judge's decision on the grounds that Article 34.4.3° necessarily extends to all decisions and verdicts of the High Court, including such decisions and verdicts as result in the acquittal of the person charged. The respondent relied on Article 38.5 of the Constitution and claimed, *inter alia*, that it asserted that no appeal lies from a verdict of 'not guilty' and that the words 'From all decisions of the High Court' in Art. 34.4.3° must be read as if such an exception applied.

Held by the Supreme Court (O'Higgins C J Walsh and Hederman JJ; Finlay P and Henchy J dissenting)
(i) That there is nothing in the Constitution which limits the provisions of Article 34.4.3° that all decisions of the High Court, except and subject as therein provided, may be appealed to the Supreme Court. Accordingly the court had jurisdiction to hear this appeal.
(ii) *Per* O'Higgins CJ the Supreme Court would not normally be concerned with verdicts of acquittal properly arrived at by a jury on their merits. Its jurisdiction would only be invoked where a mis-trial or a non trial has taken place as a result of an erroneous ruling or direction by a judge.
(iii) *Quaere per* Walsh J (a) Whether the Oireachtas is free to legislate in accordance with the provisions of Article 34 to provide that no appeal shall lie against an acquittal or that it should be only in particular circumstances. (b) Whether there is equality between the conditions of persons acquitted in the High Court and persons acquitted in the Circuit Court whose appeal procedures are entirely dependant on the provisions of the Courts of Justice Act 1924, and which are not embraced by the provisions of Article 34.

Cases referred to in judgment
Attorney General (Fahy) v Breen [1936] IR 750
Attorney General v Mallin [1957] IR 344
Bartkus v Illinois (1959) 359 US 121, 151/155
Benton v Maryland (1969) 395 US 784, 795/6
Cox v Hakes 15 AC 506
De Burca v The Attorney General [1976] IR 38
Director of Public Prosecutions v Lynch [1981] ILRM 389
In re Domvilles Estate [1930] IR 640
Fong Foo v United States (1962) 369 US 141
Great Southern and Western Railway Co v Gooding [1908] 2 IR 429
Green v United States [1957] 355 US 184, 187/188
The King (Hastings) v Justices of Galway [1906] 2 IR 499
The King (McGrath) v Chairman and Justices of Clare [1905] 2 IR 510

The People (AG) v Bell [1969] IR 24
The People (AG) v Conmey [1975] IR 341
The People (AG) v Cullen [1969] IR 24
The People (AG) v Cronin [1972] IR 159
The People (AG) v Fennell (No. 2) 1940 IR 453
The People (AG) v Kennedy [1946] IR 517
The People (AG) v Marchel O'Brien [1963] IR 65
Queen v Duncan 7 QBD 198
Queen v Justices of Antrim (1859) 2 IR 603
Queen v Russell 3 El & BL 942
Shaw v The People (DPP) [1982] IR 1
The State (AG) v Binchy [1964] IR 395
The State (Brown) v Feran [1967] IR 147
The State (Burke) v Lennon [1940] IR 136
The State (DPP) v Walsh and Keneally [1981] IR 412
In the Matter of Tilson, Infants [1951] IR 31
In re Richard Tynan Supreme Court, 1963 No. 99, 20 December 1963
In bonis Morelli: Villa v Morelli [1968] IR 11
Warner v Minister for Industry and Commerce [1929] IR 582
Wemyss v Hopkins LR 10 QB 378

Reported at [1983] ILRM 549

CRIMINAL LAW

The State (Christopher Aherne) v The Governor of Limerick Prison:
Supreme Court 1980 No. 323 (O'Higgins CJ, Walsh J, Henchy, Griffin and Hederman JJ) 21 April 1982.

Circuit Court - Appeal against conviction imposed by District Court - Whether Circuit Judge power to increase sentence - Procedure adopted in challenging Circuit Court order - Habeas corpus application - Whether well founded - Whether, despite increase in sentence, prisoner still held in accordance with law - Constitution of Ireland 1937, Art 40.4.2° - Petty Sessions Act 1851, (Ch. 93) s. 24 - Courts of Justice Act 1924, (No. 10) ss. 51, 85, 91 - Courts of Justice Act 1928, (No. 15) s. 18 - Courts (Establishment and Constitution) Act 1961, (No. 38) s. 5 - Courts (Supplemental Provisions) Act 1961, (No. 39) ss. 22(3), 22(5) (a), 48, 50 - Certiorari - Jurisdiction to grant an absolute order of certiorari at first instance - RSC O.84, rr.9, 57.

Facts The prosecutor was convicted at Cork District Court of assault and was sentenced to nine months imprisonment. He took an appeal to the Circuit Court against the conviction, the notice of appeal making no reference to sentence. In the Circuit Court the conviction was affirmed and the sentence increased to twelve months imprisonment. The prosecutor subsequently obtained a conditional order from the High Court under Article 40.4.2° of the Constitution. The Governor of the prison made a return to the order by relying on the District Court and Circuit Court orders. On the hearing of the return the High Court quashed the order of the Circuit Court on the grounds that the Circuit Court judge had no jurisdiction to increase the sentence and directed the arrest of the prosecutor, who had been released on bail, to serve the sentence imposed by the District Court ([1981] ILRM 169). The Governor appealed.

Held The Circuit Court can impose an increase of sentence on an appeal against conviction only. Order of the High Court set aside and order of Circuit Court restored.

Per Henchy and Griffin JJ. Release by way of a conditional order of habeas corpus was not open to the prosecutor. It was of the essence of his case that the nine months imprisonment which he was then serving was a proper and lawful sentence. It did not lie with him to say that he should be released on habeas corpus while that nine months sentence was being served. His complaint was that the detention would become unlawful once it came to overrun the lawful termination of the nine months term imposed in the District Court. There was also no jurisdiction to grant bail while the lawful sentence of nine months imprisonment was being served. *State (McDonagh) v Frawley* [1978] IR 131 applied.

Per Walsh and Hederman JJ. As the net point in issue had never before been decided by the Supreme Court the President of the High Court could not be faulted for having granted an order of habeas corpus because an argument was always open to the effect that the whole sentence might fall because of the alleged excess of jurisdiction. It might well be argued that the proper course would be to quash the unlawful sentence and substitute a lawful one. If the latter course were the correct one then, until that course had been followed, the detention would not be lawful.

Per Curiam. The appeal was really an appeal against an order of certiorari made by the High Court rather than against an order of habeas corpus.

Per Henchy J. Before the Circuit Court order, or any part of it, could be quashed there should have been an adjournment to enable the Circuit Court judge and the Director of Public Prosecutions to have an opportunity of opposing the quashing of the order. An absolute order of certiorari cannot be granted *ex parte*.

Per Walsh J. The application to challenge the legality of the deprivation of someone's personal liberty is enshrined as a constitutional right in respect of which the whole procedure is set out in the Constitution. It is outside the competence of any rule-making authority to make any rules whatever to regulate this procedure. Article $40.4.2°$ permits application to be made either to the High Court or to any judge thereof, but the power to order a release on the grounds that the person is not being detained in accordance with law can be exercised only by the High Court.

Cases referred to in judgment
Application of Lucey [1972] IR 347
Attorney General (Lambe) v Fitzgerald [1973] IR 195
The State (J.P. Brennan) v The Governor of Mountjoy Prison High Court, 1975 No. 7355 Finlay P, 7 May 1975
The State (McKeever) v The Governor of Mountjoy Prison Supreme Court 1965 No. 65, 19 December 1966
Ex Parte Reverend James McFadden - Habeas Corpus (Exch. Div Judgments of the

Superior Court Ireland, 1903 ed. 168, 17 May 1888)
The People v Earls [1969] IR 414
The State (McDonagh) v Frawley [1978] IR 131
The State (Royle) v Kelly [1974] IR 259
The State (Wilson) v The Governor of Portlaoise Prison, Supreme Court 1967 No. 119, 11 July 1968.
The State (Wilson) v The Governor of Portlaoise Prison, Supreme Court 1969 No. 109, 29 July 1969
R v Newcastle-under-Lyme ex parte White [1952] 2 All ER 531

Reported at [1983] ILRM 17

The State (Christopher Delaney) v District Justice Sean Magee, District Justice Sean Delap and the Governor of Mountjoy Prison: High Court 1981 No. 544SS (Gannon J) 2 April 1982.

Criminal Law - Sentence - Conviction for drunken driving - Maximum permissible sentence six months - Sentence imposed of three months imprisonment and fine of £250, with six months imprisonment in default of payment - Prosecutor therefore liable to imprisonment for nine months - Whether order made in excess of jurisdiction - Petty Sessions (Ireland) Act 1851 (Ch. 93) s. 22 - Criminal Justice Administration Act 1914, (Ch. 58) ss 3, 16 - Criminal Justice Act (No. 2) 1951, s.5 - Road Traffic Act 1961, (No.24) ss 49(2), 49(4)(a) - Road Traffic (Amendment) Act 1978 (No. 19), s 10 (4)(a) - District Court Rules r. 65.

Facts The prosecutor was convicted in the District Court of drunken driving contrary to s. 49 of the Road Traffic Act, 1961 as amended. S. 10(4)(a) of the 1978 Act allows the District Court to impose, in such cases, a maximum sentence of 6 months imprisonment and/or a maximum fine of £500. The prosecutor was sentenced to three months imprisonment and a fine of £250 with six months imprisonment in default of payment. The prosecutor applied for absolute orders of habeas corpus and certiorari on the grounds that this order was in excess of jurisdiction by making him liable to 9 months imprisonment.

Held The imprisonment for which the prosecutor could be liable in default of payment of the fine is a penalty to enforce payment and is not a punishment for the offence not is it of a category of sentence which could have exposed the prosecutor to any greater punishment than that prescribed by the Act.

Cases referred to in judgment
In Re Browne [1894] 2 IR 363
Reg. v Hopkins [1893] 1 QB 621
R v Leach Ex. p. Fritchley [1913] 3 KB 40.

Reported at [1983] ILRM 45

Director of Public Prosecutions v Stuart Clein: Supreme Court 1981 No. 218 (O'Higgins CJ, Henchy and Griffin JJ) 26 October 1982 (Nem. Diss.).

Criminal Law - Road Traffic Offence - Delay in serving summons - Date of issue altered - Whether summons invalid - Road Traffic (Amendment) Act, 1978 (No. 19) ss 12(2), 13(3).

Facts A consultative case stated from the District Court dated 13 May 1981 came before the High Court for a ruling on a legal submission made on behalf of the defendant that two summonses served on him to appear in the District Court on charges of refusing and failing to comply with the provisions of ss.12(2) and 13(3) of the Road Traffic (Amendment) Act, 1978 were invalid. The summonses were originally dated as issued on 13 July 1979 for hearing on 25 September 1979, but these dates had been altered to read 'Redated 10/10/79' and '27th day of November 1979' respectively. Both alterations were initialled by the Peace Commissioner who had issued the summonses. In the High Court Gannon J held that even if the procedure regarding the summonses were defective that was not a valid ground of defence in the circumstances. The defendant appealed.

Held Approving in full the decision of Gannon J, that the amended summonses had been served within 6 months of the making of the complaint, and it had not been shown that they were in breach of any essential requirement of the District Court Rules. Any breach of procedure was cured by the defendant's appearance in court on the day specified in the summonses. *DPP v Gill* properly distinguished by Gannon J. Appeal dismissed.

Cases referred to in judgment
DPP v Clein [1981] ILRM 465
DPP v Gill Supreme Court 1978 No. 179, 20 December 1979
The State (Attorney General) v Fawsitt [1955] IR 30

Reported at [1983] ILRM 76

The State (Rogers) v Superintendent Galvin: Supreme Court 1980 No. 300 (O'Higgins CJ, Henchy and Griffin JJ) 2 July 1982 (Nem. Diss.)

Habeas Corpus - Appearance before Special Criminal Court for purpose of charging prisoner - Application to presiding judge to sit on his own as a judge of the High Court to hear habeas corpus application - Absolute order made - Whether judge jurisdiction to make such order - Whether opportunity of justifying detention a dispensible preliminary - Waiver - Constitution of Ireland, 1937, Art. 40.4.2° - RSC O.84 rr. 2, 9.

Facts While the prosecutor, who was in the custody of the respondent, was being charged before the Special Criminal Court with capital murder the presiding judge, who was a High Court judge, acceded to a request by the prosecutor's counsel to hear a habeas corpus application immediately. The respondent was present in court in his capacity as a Garda officer. The application was opposed by the deputy assistant Chief State Solicitor who was representing the DPP. This solicitor called the respondent who gave evidence. The judge did not give the respondent any time or opportunity to do anything other than give evidence and he immediately ordered the release of the prisoner. The respondent appealed to the Supreme Court.

Held The High Court judge had failed to discharge his obligation under Art. 40.4.2° of the Constitution to give the respondent an opportunity to have legal advice and representation or to fully present his side of the case or to exercise his constitutional right to certify in writing the grounds of detention. The respondent had not effectively waived his rights. Appeal allowed.

Cases referred to in judgment
State (Aherne) v Governor of Limerick Prison [1981] ILRM 169
State (M. Woods) v Kelly [1969] IR 269
In the Matter of Zwann [1981] ILRM 333
Cases referred to in legal argument
DPP v Walsh [1980] IR 294
The People v Pringle and ors. Court of Criminal Appeal, 1980 Nos. 93, 94 and 95, 22 May 1981.
Shaw v DPP Supreme Court 1979 No. 129 (Kenny J, Walsh and Griffin JJ) 17 December 1980.
The State (Walsh) v Maguire [1979] IR 372

Reported at [1983] ILRM 149

McGlinchey v Wren: Supreme Court 1982 No. 149 (O'Higgins CJ, Henchy and Griffin JJ) 7 December 1982 (Nem. Diss.)

Extradition - Warrant for arrest issued by foreign judicial authority on a complaint of murder - Extradition order made - Application to High Court - Affidavit swearing the offence referred to was a political offence or an offence connected with a political offence - Definition of political offence - consideration of whether murder could ever be a political offence - Extradition Act, 1965 (No. 17), s. 50(2).

Facts The District Court had ordered that the plaintiff be extradited to Northern Ireland on a charge of murdering a civilian. The plaintiff had been active in the Provisional IRA which he said was primarily responsible for the murder. The plaintiff unsuccessfully applied to the High Court for an order for his release on 2 grounds, (1) that the offence was, or was connected with, a political offence; (2) that if extradited he would be charged with three other offences involving murder and unlawful possession of firearms which he alleged were, or were connected with, political offences. The plaintiff appealed to the Supreme Court where he abandoned ground 1.

Held In relation to ground 1 the murder in question could not be regarded as a political offence or an offence connected with a political offence. Whether or not an offence would be so regarded would depend on whether the person charged was at the relevant time engaged either directly or indirectly in what reasonable civilised people would regard as political activity. The judicial authorities on the scope of such offences have in many respects been rendered obsolete by the fact that modern terrorist violence is often the antithesis of what could reasonably be regarded as political. In relation to ground 2, there was no evidence that the offences in question were connected with political activity in the sense referred to in the judgment. The Supreme Court refused to assume that because of the existence of widespread violence organised by paramilitary groups in Northern Ireland, any charge associated with terrorist activity should be regarded as being in respect of an offence which was, or was connected with, a political offence. The plaintiff had failed to discharge the onus of proof and the appeal was dismissed.

No cases referred to in judgment

Reported at [1983] ILRM 169

The Director of Public Prosecutions v Patrick J. Kehoe: Court of Criminal Appeal 1981 No. 119 (McCarthy J, O'Hanlon and Murphy JJ) 7 February 1983 (Nem. Diss.)

Criminal Law - Offences against the State - Obstruction of government - Constituent ingredients of such offence - Offences against the State Act 1939, (No. 39) s. 7(1) - Criminal Law Act 1976, (No. 32) s. 2 - Diplomatic Relations and Immunities Act 1967, (No. 8) Schedule Art 22 - Evidence - Identification evidence.

Facts The appellant was convicted of an offence contrary to s. 7 of the Offences Against the State Act, 1939 as amended by s. 2 of the Criminal Law Act, 1976. The evidence given in the Special Criminal Court was that the defendant had taken part in an anti H Block demonstration outside the British Embassy. The demonstration deteriorated into a riot and a Chief Inspector of the Gardai who had been in charge of the force of Gardai assigned to protect the premises, gave evidence identifying the defendant as one who had attacked him in the course of the demonstration. On conviction he was sentenced to a term of imprisonment. The application for leave to appeal against conviction had already been dismissed by the Court of Criminal Appeal. But, as the appeal was against the first ever prosecution under s. 7 the court in a reserved judgment detailed some of its reasons for the decision.

Held (1) Without attempting to fix the bounds of the type of conduct contemplated by s. 7 of the Offences Against the State Act, 1939 the acts established against the accused constituted the offence created by the section.
(2) To constitute an offence under s. 7 it is necessary that the act complained of should constitute an attack on the State through one of its constituent organs.
(3) The terms of the section apply to the prevention or obstruction (by some violent means) of the exercise or performance of an individual legislator, judge, member of the executive or officer or employee of the State, including the Gardai and the military, of its functions, powers or duties.
(4) The section does not require that the person who is prevented or obstructed from performing his duties should have been so prevented or obstructed in the course of those duties or that the wrongdoing should have taken place with that or any other particular intent.

Case referred to in judgment
The People v Casey (No. 2) [1963] IR 33

Reported at [1983] ILRM 237

The State (Gerard O'Hagan) v District Justice Sean Delap: High Court 1982 No. 304SS (O'Hanlon J) 18 October 1982

Criminal Law - Practice - District Court - Accused electing for summary trial - Whether District Justice subsequently entitled to decline jurisdiction - Offences against the Person Act 1861 (24 & 25 Vict. c 100), s. 62 - Penal Servitude Act 1891 (54 & 55 Vict., c. 69), s. 1 - Criminal Justice Act 1951 (no. 2), ss. 2 (2)(a), 4(1)

Facts S. 2 sub-s. 2(a) of the Criminal Justice Act 1951 provides *inter alia* that the District Court may try summarily a person charged with a scheduled offence if (a) the court is of opinion that the facts proved or alleged constitute a minor offence fit to be so tried and (b) the accused does not object to being tried summarily. The prosecutor at election in the District Court before the respondent District Justice elected for summary trial on charges of indecent assault, a scheduled offence, and common assault and pleaded not guilty. The respondent accepted jurisdiction and remanded the prosecutor on bail for one week. At the request of the prosecutor's solicitor, this was altered to remand, until 2.00 pm of the same day when the prosecutor appeared for sentence before the respondent on an earlier charge of indecent assault to which he had pleaded gulty. When the matter came on, the prosecutor's solicitor informed the respondent that the prosecutor wished to change his plea to a plea of guilty on the other charges and the respondent thereupon declined jurisdiction. The prosecutor was remanded in custody to a date when he was sent forward for trial to the Dublin Circuit Court. The prosecutor applied for and got a conditional order of certiorari on the grounds that (a) the respondent having initially accepted jurisdiction was not entitled to decline it subsequently and (b) the respondent was not entitled to decline jurisdiction for reasons relating to the character of the prosecutor. The prosecutor applied to have the order made absolute and the respondent showed cause.

Held (1) Where a District Justice in the course of a summary trial comes to the conclusion on proper grounds that the matter is not one fit to be tried summarily he is entitled to discontinue the summary trial notwithstanding the fact that he had previously formed the opinion referred to in s. 2 sub-s. 2 (a) of the Act of 1951. On the facts, the trial of the prosecutor had never commenced before the decision to let the matter go forward to the Circuit Court was taken and the District Justice was not precluded from taking this course by having previously indicated an intention to allow the matter proceed on summarily trial.
(2) The presumption of innocence ceased to apply to the prosecutor when he indicated his intention to plead guilty to both sets of offences, and the respondent was faced with the prosecutor's admission that while released on bail pending sentence on a charge of indecent assault against a male person, he had committed a further similar offence against another male person. This entitled the sentence in court to regard the second offence as more serious, and could have had a material bearing on the sentence. The respondent had taken the view that a situation had arisen where the court imposing sentence should not be circumscribed by the limitation on sentencing powers of the Distirct Court and the specific facts which he took into account in forming his opinion where circumstances relating to the offence which was committed or alleged to have been committed. Accordingly, the respondent was entitled to exercise his discretion in this manner and the cause shown would be allowed.

Cases referred to in judgment
O'Leary v Cunningham [1980] IR 367
The State (Frank Clune and others) v Clifford [1981] ILRM 17
The State (Clancy) v Wine [1980] IR 228
The State (Nevin) v Tormey [1976] IR 1

Reported at [1983] ILRM 241

The Director of Public Prosecutions v Eamonn N. Kelly: 1982 No. 111 (O'Higgins CJ,Walsh J, Griffin J, Hederman and McWilliam JJ) 29 October 1982 (Nem. Diss.)

Criminal Law - Arrest under s. 30 - Whether detention in successive garda stations permitted - Conviction based on incriminating statements - finding by court of trial such statements voluntary - Approach of appeal court to such finding - Whether certain statements made in circumstances in which there was not an exact compliance with the Judges' Rules should be excluded - Whether direction to authorise continued detention valid - Courts of Justice Act 1924 (No. 10) s. 29 - Interpretation Act 1937 (No. 38) s. 11(c) - Offences against the State Act 1939 (No. 13)ss. 30(3), 30(4), 52

Facts The appellant was convicted and sentenced *in absentia* on charges of larceny and of stopping a mail train with intention to rob the mail. The only evidence against the appellant consisted of a number of verbal statements and one comprehensive written statement made while in police custody which the appellant subsequently contended had been extracted by violence and threats of violence by the interrogating Garda and/or in violation of his constitutional rights. S. 30 (3) of the Offences Against the State Act, 1939 provides *inter alia* that a person arrested under s. 30 might be removed to and detained in custody in a Garda Siochana Station, in prison or some other convenient place, for 24 hours from the time of his arrest. The appellant had been arrested on 5 April 1976 at Arklow and taken to Arklow Garda Station from whence he was removed later that morning to Fitzgibbon Street Garda Station in Dublin and shortly after midnight to the Bridewell Garda Station. The appellant appealed to the Court of Criminal Appeal having upon appeal to the Supreme Court obtained an enlargement of time for this purpose, but the appeal was dismissed. Leave to appeal was refused but the Court of Criminal Appeal certified that the application involved a point of law of exceptional public importance, i.e. whether a person arrested under s. 30 and detained in a particular Garda Station and then transferred to another Garda Station ceased by reason of that transfer to be in lawful custody.

Held (O'Higgins CJ, Walsh, Griffin, Hederman, McWilliam JJ) (i) The subsection must be strictly construed and its primary purpose was to authorise a post-arrest detention for a specified period and as long as the duration of the detention was within the permitted period and for the purpose of removel to or in a place complying within the sub-section it was permitted and plurality of such places or of removals thereto did not contravene the sub-section; (ii) On the evidence, the Court of Criminal Appeal was correct in regarding the decision of the Court of Trial on the issue of facts surrounding the making of the various statements as one which should not be disturbed. *People v Madden* applied, *Reg. v Cooper* disapproved; (iii) Statements made in answer to questions put by a member of the Gardai when the accused was in custody were not to be excluded on that ground alone (*AG v Galvin* applied). S. 30 of the 1939 Act permits the questioning of a person detained subject to qualification mentioned in *People v Madden*. (iv) Appeal dismissed.

Cases referred to in judgment
Attorney General v McCabe (1) [1927] IR 129
Director of Public Prosecutions v Eamonn N. Kelly Court of Criminal Appeal 1981 No. 72 (Finlay P) 2 April 1982 and extracts from Finlay P's judgment reported at [1983] ILRM281
Northern Bank Finance Corporation Ltd v Gerard Charleton and Others [1979] IR 149
The People (Attorney General) v Galvin [1964] IR 325
The People v Madden [1977] IR 336
The People v McNally and Breathnach Court of Criminal Appeal 1978 No. 103 (Finlay P, Henchy and Barrington JJ) 16 February 1981

Regina v Cooper (Sean) [1969] 1 QBD 267
Regina v Turnbull & Anor [1976] 3 WLR 445
The Queen v Johnston 15 Ir. CLR 60

Reported at [1983] ILRM 271

The State (Samuel Williams) v The Director of Public Prosecutions and District Justice Humphrey Kelleher: High Court 1982 No 66SS (O'Hanlon J) 20 July 1982

Criminal Law - Procedure - Preliminary examination - Whether proceedings marked by such irregularities as to justify High Court intervening by way of prohibition - Charge not giving particulars of time or place at which alleged offence was committed - Accused not served with list of witnesses or with a statement of the evidence - Failure by District Justice to warn witness about self incriminatory answers - Whether such failure could be relied on by accused - Criminal Procedure Act 1865 (28 Vict. c. 18), ss 1, 3, 4, 5 - Criminal Procedure Act 1967 (12), ss. 6(1), 7(2) - District Court Rules 1967 (SI No. 181), 5

Director of Public Prosecutions - Preliminary Examination - Undertaking that evidence given would not be used for the purpose of criminal proceedings against witness - effect of such undertaking

Facts The prosecutor was charged by summons with conspiring to defraud the Revenue Commissioners and appeared before the second named respondent District Justice at Killarney District Court where a statement of charge defectively reproducing the contents of the summons was served upon him. The prosecutor was not served with a list of the witnesses proposed to be called at the trial or with a statement of the evidence to be given by each of them. His solicitor was subsequently informed that a deposition of the evidence of one witness was to be taken at the preliminary examination. This witness was not cautioned by the second named respondent in terms that he was not obliged to answer questions if the answers might tend to incriminate him, although the first named respondent had undertaken that evidence so given for use against the prosecutor would not be used in criminal proceedings against this witness. The second named respondent subsequently allowed the first named respondent to cross examine their own witness when called to make the sworn deposition and allowed him to be questioned about a previous statement in writing alleged to be inconsistent with evidence given in direct examination. The prosecutor applied for and got a conditional order of prohibition prohibiting the respondents from proceeding further with the preliminary examination of the criminal charge and the prosecutor now applied to have the order made absolute.

Held (i) The statement of charge although prepared in a careless or slip-shod manner passed muster under s. 6 sub-s. 1(a) of the Criminal Procedure Act, 1967 since it could be clearly identified by the prosecutor as being the same charge referred to in the summons.

(ii) The failure to serve the necessary documents specified in s. 6 sub-s 1 of the Act was a matter to be considered by the second named respondent when making his adjudication as to whether he should send the accused forward for trial, and the point of such adjudication had not yet been reached. Although the time prescribed by the District Court Rules 1967 within which these documents were to be served on the accused had long expired, the prosecution could still apply for an extension of time for their service.

(iii) The failure of the second named respondent to caution the witness, while it might give rise to a cause for complaint on the part of the witness himself, was not a circumstance that could be relied upon by the prosecutor as a ground for seeking protection.

(iv) The general rule applying in other criminal and civil proceedings relating to a witness who proved adverse or hostile applies with equal force in the course of the preliminary investigation carried out by a District Justice pursuant to the provisions of the Criminal Procedure Act 1967, and in the present case the second named respondent had acted within his proper jurisdiction in permitting the witness to be cross examined as to a previous inconsistent statement made by him.

Conditional Order discharged.

Cases referred to in judgment
People (Attorney General) v Taylor [1974] IR 97
The State (Bachelor & Co Ltd) v O'Floinn [1958] IR 155
Clune and Ors v Director of Public Prosecutions [1981] ILRM 17
The State (Healy) v Donoghue and Ors [1976] IR 325
The State (Hogan) v Carroll [1981] ILRM 25
Lawder v Lawder 5 Ir CLR 27, 473
Nunn v Walsh (1849)
R v Gee and Ors 25 CAR 198
R v Phillips and Anor 26 CAR 200
R v Smyth 2 Stark
R v Walker 34 CAR 199
R v Wharmoy 31 CAR 174
Rice v Howard 16 QBD 681
The State (Shannon) v O'hUadhaigh [1975] IR 98

The State (Williams) v The DPP and Kelleher
The High Court judgment of this case was reported in issue no. 7 ILRM.
On appeal to the Supreme Court the appeal was allowed and the conditional order of prohibition was made absolute.

Reported at [1983] ILRM 285

The State (Patrick Laffey) v His Honour Judge John Grattan Esmonde, The Director of Public Prosecutions and The Governor of Mountjoy Prison: Supreme Court 1978 No. 216 (O'Higgins CJ, Henchy and Griffin JJ) 2 July 1982.

Criminal Law - Procedure - Young Person - Plea of guilty - Circuit Court Judge certifying that defendant not a fit person to be detained in a place of detention for young persons - Whether court then entitled to impose such punishment as the law provides and the Court thinks proper - Children Act 1908 (Ch.67), ss, 101(3), 102(3), 106, 131 - Children Act 1941(No.12),s. 29.

Facts The prosecutor, aged 15, signed plea of guilty in Galway District Court and was sent forward to Circuit Court for sentence. Sentenced to two years' imprisonment in Mountjoy by Judge Grattan Esmonde who certified that he was of unruly and depraved character and unfit to be detained in a place of detention for young persons. Prosecutor obtained conditional orders of certiorari and Habeas Corpus on basis that sentence was contrary to the Children Act, 1908. Cause was shown but orders made absolute in High Court, Appeal to Supreme Court.

Held By O'Higgins CJ, allowing the appeal and discharging the orders: That s. 102 sub-s. 3 of the 1908 Act provides that a young person may be sentenced to imprisonment provided that the court certifies that he is of unruly and depraved character and unfit to be detained in a place of detention for young persons. S. 106 of the Act, which limits the sentence to one month's duration does not apply, as the effect of the section is limited to circumstances when 'the court considers that none of the other methods whereby the case can be dealt with is suitable'. Henchy J and Griffin J concurred.

No cases referred to in judgment

Reported at [1983] ILRM 291

The State (Sylvester Higgins) v Superintendent N. M. Reid: High Court 1981 No412SS (Barrington J) 29 July 1982

Criminal Law - Road Traffic - Drunken driving - Refusal to supply copy of the certificate completed by designated registered medical practitioner - Whether obligation to supply copy of documentary evidence in advance of the hearing - Road Traffic Act 1961 (No. 24) s. 10 - Road Traffic (Amendment) Act, 1978 (No. 19) ss. 21(1), 21(4), 22(3)

61

Facts Prosecutor arrested under s. 10 of 1961 Act (as amended), taken to Garda Station and introduced to medical practitioner. Invited to give blood sample, but he did not understand name of the doctor. His solicitor applied to the Garda for copy of the doctor's certificate in advance of the hearing to enable him to prepare defence. This was refused by respondent, who indicated that the certificate would be available to prosecutor for perusal at the District Court hearing. Conditional order of mandamus to compel production of certificate in advance of hearing granted. Cause shown.

Held by Barrington J, allowing the cause shown and discharging the conditional order: that the matter of determining whether the fair administration of justice requires that the accused should or should not be furnished with the certificate is essentially one for the court before which the prosecution is pending. Accordingly, it would not be appropriate for the High Court to intervene.

Case referred to in judgment
Clune and Ors. v Director of Public Prosecutions [1981] ILRM 17

Reported at [1983] ILRM 310

In the Matter of a Prosecution Pending in the District Court:
In the Matter of an Application for an Order of Attachment for Contempt of Court against An Taoiseach, Charles J. Haughey Esq. TD: The Owners and Editor of the Irish Press and the Owners and Editor of the Sunday World: Malcolm Edward Daniel MacArthur — Applicant. High Court 1982 No. 474 SS (Costello J) 1 September 1982.

Criminal Law - Contempt - Ex Parte application by accused - Inadvertent comment - Immediate steps taken to avoid any possible prejudice - Taoiseach receiving letter from accused - Taoiseach authorizing publication in the National Press - Photograph of accused published - Whether contempt of court.

Facts The applicant was arrested and charged with a criminal offence. Before his trial, the applicant made an *ex parte* application to the High Court on the grounds that the respondents had been guilty of criminal contempt in the making and publication of certain statements and in the publication of a photograph all of which might be likely to prejudice the due course of justice.

The applicant alleged that the Taoiseach, Charles J. Haughey had committed an offence on 17 August 1982 by using certain words which admittedly had been spoken inadvertently in the course of a press conference. It had been necessary to use the words complained of to answer questions, some of which touched on the applicant's forthcoming trial. However, the Government Information Service had then requested journalists not to report the remarks. It was also alleged that the Taoiseach had committed an offence on 18 August 1982 by causing to be published in the Irish Press part of the contents of a letter which had allegedly been sent to him by the applicant. The applicant also sought conditional orders against the editor and proprietor of the Irish Press in relation to the publication on 19 and 20 August 1982 relating to a letter alleged to have been written by the applicant to the Attorney General. The applicant also complained that the publication in the Irish Press on 18 August of information relating to items of evidence found in the flat in which the accused had been arrested constituted an act of contempt. The applicant's final complaint was against the editor and proprietors of Sunday World which had published a photograph of the applicant on 22 August 1982. It was submitted that the publication constituted contempt because the question of the visual identification of the applicant could be an issue at his trial. Publication had occurred after a statement had been issued by the Director of Public Prosecutions that an investigation was being held into media coverage relating to the applicant as well as into possible future coverage relating to the applicant.

Held by Costello J:
 (i) That the applicant had failed to establish a prima facie case against either An Taoiseach, Charles J. Haughey or against the Irish Press.
 (ii) The applicant had established a prima facie case against the Sunday World. *Semble.* As the Director of Public Prosecutions was already investigating possible contempts of court the application against the Sunday World was adjourned with liberty to re-enter when the Director had indicated what steps he proposed to take in the light of the investigation.

Cases referred to in judgment
Keegan v De Burca [1973] IR 223 at 227
R v Evening Standard Company [1954] 1 QB 578
Director of Public Prosecutions v Walsh and Conneely Unreported 6 February 1981.

Reported at [1983] ILRM 355

The Director of Public Prosecutions v Philip McPartland: High Court 1982 No. 398SS (O'Hanlon J) 17 January 1983

Criminal Law - Practice - Road Traffic Offence - Misdescription of accused in Medical Bureau Certificate - Whether sufficient evidence - Whether accused the person named on the certificate - Road Traffic Act 1961 (No. 24) ss. 49(2), 49(4)(a) - Road Traffic Amendment Act 1978 (No. 19) s. 10

Facts The defendant was charged in the District Court with offences under s. 49 sub-s. 2 and 4(a) of the Road Traffic Act, 1961 as inserted by s. 10 of the Road Traffic (Amendment) Act, 1978. The charges were dismissed by the District Justice on the ground that the medical certificate on which the prosecution case depended had an incorrect address, and consequently there was no evidence that the defendant was the person named in the certificate. Pursuant to s. 51 of the Courts (Supplemental) Provisions Act, 1961, the district justice then stated a case to the High Court, paragraph 7 of which was as follows:

> The opinion of the court is sought as to whether I [the District Justice] was right in law in dismissing the said complaint.

Held The summons in response to which the defendant appeared at the hearing bore the same address as the certificate. No objection was taken to those wrong particulars nor was amendment of them sought at the hearing. The matter was to be remitted to the District Court as the District Justice had erred in law in finding that there was no evidence that the defendant was the person named in the medical certificate.

No cases referred to in judgment

Reported at [1983] ILRM 411

The State (Thomas McDonagh) v District Justice J. Barry: High Court 1981 No. 505SS (Gannon J) 22 November 1982.

Criminal Law - District Court prosecution - Plea of guilty - Legal aid denied - Charges not stated to accused in open court - Application for certiorari to quash conviction - Whether District Court orders good on their face - Whether orders made without or in excess of jurisdiction - Malicious Damage Act 1861(Ch97)s. 52 - Larceny Act 1916 (C. 50), s. 23(a) - Criminal Justice Act 1951 (No. 2), ss. 2, 8 - Criminal Procedure Act 1967 (No. 12), s. 13(2)(b) - Criminal Law (Jurisdiction) Act 1976, (No.14), s. 6 - District Court Rules 1972, rr. 84, 85

Facts The prosecutor was arrested and charged on 29 September 1981 with entering as a trespasser and stealing money from a house in Ballymote. Most of the stolen money was later recovered. The prosecutor was remanded to Sligo District Court and brought before the respondent District Justice on 2 October 1981 where he elected to be tried by a judge and jury. The case was then adjourned for a week and the prosecutor remanded to Mountjoy prison from whence he applied for legal aid and wrote to the Gardai indicating a wish to have his trial disposed of summarily. On 9 October 1981 the prosecutor applied to the respondent for legal aid but was refused. None of the charges were read to the prosecutor on this occasion. The respondent thereafter, but without being informed of the letter written to the Gardai, heard the facts of the case and imposed sentences of four months in respect of each charge to run concurrently. The respondent later recalled the prosecutor and asked whether he wished to have the charges dealt with by the respondent or by judge and jury to which the prosecutor replied by the respondent and the respondent confirmed the sentences already imposed. The prosecutor applied for and obtained a conditional order of certiorari on the grounds that (a) the prosecutor was denied legal aid, (b) there was an absence of jurisdiction and (c) that the hearing on 9 October 1981 did not proceed in due course of law. The respondent contended on the facts that the prosecutor had agreed in court to be dealt with by the District Court and that he had been asked whether he wished to have the charges read over to him. The prosecutor applied to have the order made absolute.

Held The procedure in Sligo District Court on the evidence was irregular since *inter alia* (i) the prosecutor's application for legal aid had been considered before a statement was taken of the facts required for a determination under s. 2 of the Criminal Justice Act 1951. (ii) This was followed by sentence without any opportunity for the prosecutor to say anything on his own behalf in relation to sentence. (iii) The charges had not been put to the prosecutor in court and the consideration required by s. 2 of the 1951 Act if made at all was only made after the sentences had been imposed. (iv) It was clear that the prosecutor had no clear idea of the charges to which the sentences related, and the respondent had no knowledge of the letter written by the prosecutor from Mountjoy prison nor was he informed that most of the stolen money had been recovered by the Gardai. Accordingly on the facts everything about the way the proceedings went demonstrated that the prosecutor should have had the assistance of a legal advisor. Conditional Order made absolute.

No cases referred to in judgment

Reported at [1983] ILRM 525

The State (Samuel Williams) v Director of Public Prosecutions and District Justice Humphrey Kelliher: Supreme Court 1982 No. 223 (Henchy J, Griffin and McCarthy JJ) 27 July 1983

Criminal Law - Procedure - Preliminary examination - Statement of charge not setting out the time or place of the alleged offence - Failure to serve Book of Evidence - Application for an order of prohibition - Effect of non-compliance with statutory requirements - Whether objection to District Justice's jurisdiction be postponed - Criminal Procedure Act 1967, (No. 12), ss. 5, 6, 8 -

Facts The prosecutor was charged by summons with conspiring to defraud the Revenue Commissioners and appeared before the second named respondent in the District Court where a statement of charge defectively reproducing the contents of the summons was served upon him. The second named respondent commenced, under the Criminal Procedure Act 1967, (hereinafter referred to as 'the Act'), a preliminary investigation of the alleged offence. The prosecutor was not served with a list of the witnesses whom it was proposed to call at the trial or a statement of the evidence to be given by each of them even though section 6 sub-s. 1 of the Act requires such service. The representative of the first named respondent called one witness a certain Thomas Healy to give a deposition as to the preliminary investigation. The second named respondent allowed the representative of the first named respondent to cross examine Healy as a hostile witness after it was proved that he had given evidence inconsistent with a previous written statement made to the Revenue Commissioners. The prosecutor obtained a conditional order of prohibition prohibiting the respondents from proceeding further with the preliminary investigation. The High Court (O'Hanlon J) refused to make absolute the conditional order and discharged it, holding (*inter alia*) that the statement of charge, though incomplete, could clearly be identified by the prosecutor as being the same charge as that in the summons. O'Hanlon J also held that the failure to serve the documents specified in section 6 sub-s. 1 of the Act was a matter to be considered by the second named respondent when making his adjudication under s. 8 of the Act as to whether the prosecutor should be sent forward for trial. Because the point of such adjudication had not been reached, O'Hanlon J held that it would be premature to make any order preventing any future adjudication. He also held that the second named respondent had been within his jurisdiction in allowing Healy to be cross examined as a hostile witness. See [1983] ILRM 285. The prosecutor appealed to the Supreme Court against the discharge of the conditional order.

Held per Henchy J (with whom Griffin and McCarthy JJ agreed). Because s. 5 sub-s. 1 of the Act stipulates that the District Justice 'shall conduct a preliminary examination of the charge in accordance with this part' (i.e. Part 2 ss. 5 to 20), there cannot be a valid preliminary examination if the requirements of section 6 sub-s. 1 are not, at least substantially, complied with. The failure to serve what is usually called the book of evidence was a substantial and crucial failure by the prosecution to comply with the requirements of section 6 sub-s. 1 and this failure deprives the District Justice of jurisdiction to enter on the preliminary investigation of the offence charged. O'Hanlon J had been incorrect in holding that the objection to the second named respondent's jurisdiction should be postponed until the time for an adjudication under s. 8 of the Act as to whether the prosecutor be sent for trial because such an adjudication is concerned with the question whether there is 'a sufficient case to put the accused on trial for the offence with which he has been charged' and not the question whether the pretrial statutory requirements of adducing evidence against the prosecutor were complied with. The prosecutor's complaint of absence of jurisdiction was well founded and was not premature. The omissions in the statement of charge might have been overlooked if the other requirements of s. 6 sub-s. 1 had been complied with. The appeal was allowed and an absolute order of prohibition restraining the further conduct of this preliminary examination for want of prior compliance with the requirements of s. 6 sub-s. 1 of the Act was granted.

Per Griffin J (with whom McCarthy J agreed). It might have been legitimate to allow Healy to be treated as a hostile witness if a statement of the evidence to be given by him had been served under s. 6 sub-s. 1 (d)

Reported at [1983] ILRM 537

The People (Director of Public Prosecutions) v Patrick Leo O'Shea:
Supreme Court 1980 No. 190 (No. 2) (O'Higgins CJ, Finlay P, Walsh J, Henchy and McCarthy JJ) 6 May 1983 (Nem. Diss.)

Criminal Law - Acquittal by direction of trial judge - Appeal to Supreme Court - Appeal dismissed - Reasons

Facts In the Central Criminal Court the respondent was charged with certain offences. On the direction of the trial judge the jury found him not guilty on all counts preferred against him. The appellants appealed to the Supreme Court against his acquittal. The circumstances relating to the respondent's indictment were as follows. In August, 1979 three men were arrested by Gardai and charged with offences contrary to the Misuse of Drugs Act, 1977. The respondent was not one of them. Some days later the respondent instructed his solicitor that he wished to make a statement to certain named members of the Garda Siochana. He then volunteered a lengthy statement to the Gardai in which he alleged that he had been innocently involved in an incident with drugs which had occurred some days before. The statement was the only evidence associating him with the incident. At the trial a Garda witness said that he was satisfied that the facts as related were accurate and that the respondent had been telling the truth. The trial judge then directed the jury to find the respondent not guilty on the basis that there was insufficient proof to secure a conviction.

Held by the Supreme Court (O'Higgins CJ, Finlay P, Walsh, Henchy and McCarthy JJ) in dismissing the appeal
There was insufficient evidence to have permitted the case to go to the jury.
Reported at [1983] ILRM 591

FAMILY LAW

CP v DP: High Court 1981 No. 921sp (Finlay P) 27 May 1982.

Husband and Wife - Claim for transfer of ownership of family home - Husband substantially in debt - Deposit of title deeds by way of equitable mortgage - Whether husband engaged in such conduct as might lead to the loss of the family home - Whether husband any intention of depriving the wife of residence - Meaning of intention - Claim for maintenance - Family Home Protection Act 1976, (No. 27) s. 5(1).

Facts The evidence at the hearing established that the defendant deposited the title deeds of the family home with a bank as security for an overdraft, and that he also had certain other substantial unsecured debts. The plaintiff alleged that the defendant's conduct was such as could lead to the loss of the family home with the intention of depriving the wife and dependent children of their residence in it. It was also claimed that the provisions of s. 5 sub-s. 1 of the Family Home

Protection Act, 1976 then became operative thereby vesting in the court a discretionary power to direct the husband to transfer the legal ownership in the family home to the plaintiff wife. The question to be determined was whether on the evidence the court would be entitled to hold, in the words of s. 5 sub-s. 1, that the husband was 'engaging in such conduct as may lead to the loss of any interest in the family home . . . with the intention of depriving the applicant spouse or a dependent child of the family of his residence in the family home'. It was submitted that the word 'intention' should be construed as not being equivalent with motive, but rather with the 'intention' which could be imputed to any person as to the natural and probable consequences of their conduct.

Held 1. Before a court can construe the word 'intention' in s. 5 sub-s. 1 as being equivalent to the implied or imputed intention which can arise from the natural and probably consequences of an act or omission, there must first be an element of deliberate conduct involved.

2. The evidence could not sustain the assertion that the defendant's actions constituted sufficient deliberateness to establish an intention to present a risk to the loss of an interest in the family home.

Cases referred to in judgment
Containercare v W. and Another High Court 1981 No. 341 sp (Carroll J) 25 November 1981
D v D High Court (Cosetllo J) 16 December 1981
Reported at [1983] ILRM 380

S v S: High Court 1982 No. 862 Sp. (McWilliam J) 3 February 1983.

Husband and Wife - Family Home - Wife seeking order transferring ownership of family home - Husband acting improvidently and incurring substantial debts - Whether husband any intention of depriving wife of residence - Meaning of intention - Family Home Protection Act 1976 (No. 27) s. 5(1).

Facts The plaintiff wife sought *inter alia* an order pursuant to s. 5 sub-s. 1 of the Family Home Protection Act 1976 transferring the family home to her sole name. The family home was purchased in 1977 in the joint names of both spouses. In June 1982 the plaintiff first learned of her husband's severe financial difficulties from a creditor who informed her that the house would have to be sold. Some days later the defendant husband disappeared, and the evidence suggested that he had left the country. Substantial claims against the defendant for accumulated debts by various creditors remained outstanding in addition to a pending investigation with regard to possible criminal offences against him.

The question for the determination of the court was whether in the light of the s. 5 sub-s. 1 of the 1976 Act the plaintiff was now entitled to the transfer order sought.

Held by McWilliam J in dismissing the claim. While the conduct of the defendant might have been improvident and possibly dishonest it did not disclose an outright intention of depriving the plaintiff and children of their residence in the family home as required by the provisions of s. 5 sub-s. 1 in order to maintain a valid claim for a transfer of the defendant's interest in the family home. *ED v FD* High Court 23 October applied.

Cases referred to in judgment
ED v FD High Court 1979 No. 26 Sp. (Costello J) 23 October 1980.
O'M v O'M High Court (Finlay P) 21 December 1981.
CP v DP [1982] ILRM XXX
Reported at [1983] ILRM 387

INJUNCTIONS

The Attorney General at the Relation of Francis X Martin v Dublin Corporation and The Commissioners of Public Works in Ireland: Supreme Court 1981 No. 68 (O'Higgins CJ, Walsh J, Henchy J, Griffin and McMahon JJ) 16 February 1983 (Nem. Diss)

Injunction - Fiat of Attorney General secured - Injunction granted on undertaking to abide by any order as to damages - Fiat not extending to this undertaking - Error in High Court record - Whether plaintiffs able to rely on this - Whether Attorney General liable in respect of plaintiff's loss
Attorney General - Role of Attorney General in relation to proceedings

Facts The Relator in the proceedings Fr F. X. Martin had sought an injunction restraining the defendant from building on the Wood Quay site which had been declared a national monument, without a valid consent under the National Monuments Act 1930. He also sought a declaration that the consent upon which the Corporation purported to act were of no legal effect. To bring such a claim in the High Court it was necessary for him to secure the Fiat of the Attorney General. This Fiat was given on the basis that Fr. Martin would pay the Attorney General the costs and expenses and on the understanding that the Attorney General expressed no opinion on the legal issues involved. The action then proceeded as a relator action with the Attorney General named as plaintiff 'At the Relation of Francis X. Martin'. On 10 January 1979 counsel for Fr Martin obtained an interim order in the High Court restraining the defendants carrying on further works on the Wood Quay site. The order was given on the basis of an undertaking given on Fr. Martin's behalf that he would abide by any order the court might later award to the defendant for any damages suffered as a result of the plaintiff's action. Counsel for Fr. Martin also informed the court that the Attorney General's Fiat did not extend to or include such an undertaking. However, the actual wording of the interim order recited that the undertaking had been given by the plaintiff (the Attorney General) by his Counsel. The Attorney General did not appear at any stage in the proceedings, nor was he represented at such. Further errors had appeared in the order of the Supreme Court when the interlocutory order was discharged and the matter was remitted to the High Court 'for an assessment of the damages in pursuance of the undertaking given by the plaintiff F. X. Martin'. Counsel for the Corporation submitted that (i) The orders should be accepted as they stood and that the Attorney General as plaintiff should be liable for damages. (ii) That in the alternative, the Attorney General had impliedly accepted a joint and several liability to pay damages.

Held (1) While the Attorney General was clearly the plaintiff in relator proceedings it was not he who had given the undertaking.
2) The giving of the Attorney General's consent does not necessarily indicate his approval of the proceedings. This had been expressed on his behalf when the proceedings had commenced.
(3) The acceptance or otherwise of an undertaking was a matter for the court. The trial judge had exercised his discretion in declining to seek an undertaking as to damages from or a lodgment of such by the Attorney General.
(4) Appeal dismissed.

Case referred to in judgment
Attorney General (Humphries) v Governors of Erasmus Smith Schools [1910] 1 IR 325

Reported at [1983] ILRM 254

Campus Oil Ltd, Estuary Fuel Ltd, McMullan Bros. Ltd, Ola Teo., PMPA Oil Company Ltd and Tedcastle McCormick and Co Ltd v The Minister for Industry and Energy, Ireland, The Attorney General and Irish National Petroleum Corporation Ltd: High Court 1982 No. 9256P (Murphy J)22 September 1982

European Economic Community - Supply and distribution of fuel - Government powers to regulate acquisition, supply, distribution and marketing - Whether incomplete with Community obligations - Whether mandatory regime a quantitative restriction or measure having equivalent effect - Whether restriction on competition - Application for interlocutory injunction - Whether injunction be granted. Treaty of Rome, Articles 30, 31, 36, 85, 86, 90 - Fuels (Controls of Supplies) Act 1971 (No. 3) ss. 2, 3 - Fuels (Controls of Supplies) Act 1982 (No. 18) s. 3(1) - Fuels (Control of Supplies) Order 1982

Injunction - Interlocutory - Principles to be applied - Disputed facts - Serious questions of law raised demanding detailed argument - balance of convenience - Whether injunction be granted.

Facts The plaintiff Irish controlled companies imported petroleum products for sale in the State. In August 1982 the Minister for Industry and Energy made an order under s. 3 of the Fuels (Control of Supplies) Act 1971 as amended directing *inter alia* that the plaintiffs purchase up to a maximum of 35% of their requirements of petroleum oil or 40% of any particular type of petroleum oil from the fourth named defendant which, but for the order, the plaintiffs could otherwise have bought elsewhere. The order further empowered the Minister to determine the price of the petroleum oil so purchased. The plaintiffs claimed a declaration that the order was invalid and on the grounds that (i) it was inconsistent with Articles, 30, 31, 85, 86 and 90 of the Treaty of Rome and (ii) contravened Articles 40 and 43 of the Constitution. The plaintiffs sought an interlocutory injunction restraining the defendants from implementing the provisions of the 1982 order pending the determination of the proceedings and relied for this application on the provisions of the Treaty of Rome rather than upon the Constitution. Articles 30 and 31 of the Treaty prohibit quantitive restrictions on imports between member states. The plaintiffs contended that the 1982 order constituted a quantitative restriction or a measure having equivalent effect. The defendants relied on Article 36 which permits restrictions on imports justified on grounds of public security, contending that it was essential for the State to have a substantial national refining capacity in order to maintain national and economic security. The plaintiffs further contended that since the fourth named defendant was an undertaking its agreement to co-operate with the regime constituted by the order would enfringe the competition rules of the Common Market under Article 85 of the Treaty.

Held The distinction drawn between the judgments in *American Cyanamid Co v Ethicon Ltd* and *Educational Company of Ireland Ltd v Fitzpatrick and Others* are more apparent than real. A litigant seeking an interlocutory injunction must be able to show a fair *prima facie* case in support of the title he asserts. The defendants case required investigation of a complex area of economics and international commerce and required a determination of serious questions of law both national and international. It was accordingly not possible to decide on the strengths of the plaintiffs case nor upon its prospects for success and on the evidence, the frustration of the Minister's proposals even temporarily would prejudice the public interest and cause loss which could not be compensated for in money. Accordingly the balance of convenience favoured withholding of an injunction. Motion refused.

Cases referred to in judgment
American Cyanamid Company v Ethicon Ltd [1975] AC 396
Dublin Port and Docks Board v Britannia Dredging Co. Ltd [1968] IR 136
The Educational Company of Ireland Ltd v Fitzpatrick and Others [1961] IR 323
General Motors Continental NV v Commission of the European Community [1975] 2 ECR 1367
Ministere Public of Luxembourg v Heinn Muller and Others [1971] ECR 723
De Peijper [1976] ECR 613
Procureur du Roi v Dassonville [1974] 2 ECR 837

Reported at [1983] ILRM 258   (Appeal to the Supreme Court dismissed.)

Harry Fleming and Others v Ranks (Ireland) Ltd and Donal O'Donoghue
High Court 1983 No. 1349P (McWilliam J) 16 March 1983

Injunction - Interlocutory - Mareva Injunction - Whether jurisdiction to grant such an injunction - Whether confined to cases where defendant is resident outside the State - Whether real risk of removal or disposal of defendant's assets - Balance of convenience - Judicature (Ireland) Act 1877 (Ch. 57) s. 28 (8)

Facts In 1978 an agreement was made between the Irish Transport and General Workers Union (The Union) and Ranks Ireland Ltd the first named defendants. The union was expressed to be acting on behalf of its members attached to Ranks Dublin North City Mill and a schedule to the agreement set out details of compensation for various categories of employees made redundant. In October, 1982 Ranks made certain redundancy proposals which proved to be unacceptable to the union. The matter was then referred to the Labour Court which by determination made on 7 January 1983 made certain recommendations which were unacceptable to Ranks. When the union issued strike notice Ranks announced that the Mills in Dublin and Limerick would have to close on 4 February 1983. Further meetings took place which resulted in proposals which were accepted by a majority of the members of the union. However, this decision was not accepted by the plaintiffs who in due course sought an interlocutory injunction restraining the defendants from disposing of or dealing with the assets of Ranks (Ireland) Ltd so as to reduce the value thereof below the sum of £83,724.92: so as to evade any obligation to the plaintiffs. It was then submitted on their behalf that the court should take account of the behaviour of the plaintiffs who in occupying the defendant's premises had taken active steps to prevent Ranks from properly preserving large quantities of wheat and flour which constituted substantial though perishable assets of the company.

Held by McWilliam J:
1. Although the court would not ordinarily grant an injunction to restrain a defendant from parting with his assets so that they may be preserved in case the plaintiffs' claim succeeds, the court does have jurisdiction to grant an injunction to restrain the removal of assets out of the jurisdiction or the disposal of them in the jurisdiction if the anticipated removal or disposal, is for the practice of preventing the plaintiff with a good arguable case recovering damages.
2. The cases in which such an injunction may be granted are not confined to cases in which the defendant is resident outside the State.
3. Although the plaintiffs had a good arguable case, and there was a danger of default through inability to pay damages, an injunction could only be granted if any anticipated disposal of the defendant's assets was for the purpose of preventing a plaintiff to recover damages and not merely for the purpose of carrying on a business or discharging lawful debts.

Cases referred to in judgment
American Cynnamid Co v Ethicon Ltd [1975] AC 396; [1975] 2 WLR 316

Barclay-Johnson v Yuill [1980] 1 WLR 1259
Goulding Chemicals Limited v Bolger [1977] IR 211
Mareva Compania Naviera SA v International Bulkcarriers SA [1975] 2 Lloyd's Rep. 509 and [1980] 1 All ER 213n CA
Lister & Co. v Stubbs (1890) 45 Ch. D. 1 CA
Rahman v Abu-Taha [1980] 1 WLR 1268
Rasu Maritima SA v Perusahaan Pertambangan Minyak Dan Gas Bumi Negera [1978] QB 644; [1977] 3 WLR 518
Searose Ltd v Seatrain UK Ltd [1981] QB 923; [1981] 2 WLR 601.
Z Ltd v AZ and AA-LL [1982] 2 WLR 288

Reported at [1983] ILRM 541

INTERNATIONAL LAW

Laurence O'Daly and Marie Claude Reverte v Gulf Oil Terminals (Ireland) Ltd, Gulf Oil Corporation and Total Compagnie Francaise De Navigation: High Court 1981 No. 14100P (Barrington J) 7 July 1982.

Conflict of laws - Fatal damages claim - Victims using French nationals employed on French registered ship employed under French contracts of service - Motion to set aside order authorising the institution of proceedings - Explosion occurring on board the vessel but within Irish waters - Whether occurring on French national territory - Whether Irish courts should decline jurisdiction in favour of French courts - RSC O. 12 r. 26

Facts On January 8 1979 at the Oil Terminal at Whiddy Island Bantry County Cork a motor vessel owned by the third named defendant blew up killing 37 people including its entire crew. The terminal and jetty were owned and occupied by the first named defendants. The first named plaintiff to the within proceedings was the administrator of the Estate of and the second named plaintiff was the widow of a crew member who died in the tragedy. The third named defendant applied to the court pursuant to order 12 r. 26, to set aside an order authorising the institution of proceedings against the defendants and the service of notice thereof on the third named defendant outside the jurisdiction on the grounds that *inter alia* the Irish courts had no jurisdiction to try the case, since the victims were French nationals employed under French contracts of service, the ship was a French registered ship which was French territory governed by French law, or, alternatively, if the Irish courts had jurisdiction to try the case they should in their discretion decline jurisdiction since *inter alia* every seaman employed on board a French ship was subject to French maritime law and was affiliated to a social security system which in the event of death would result in payment being made as of right to his dependants. The plaintiffs contended that having regard to the comparative costs and convenience of proceedings including the availability of witnesses it would be preferable to have the case tried in Ireland. The first named defendants wished to have the matter determined in Ireland, the second named defendants reserving their position.

Held For the third named defendant to succeed it would be necessary for them to show that the fact that a private ship was registered in France and flew the French flag would oust the jurisdication of the littoral state in whose waters the ship happened to be. The domestic courts in accordance with principals of international law will accord to the ship and its crew and contents certain immunities which immunities do not depend upon an objective extra-territoriality but on implication of the domestic law. They are conditional and in any case can be waived by the nation to which the public ship belongs. (*Chung Chi Cheung v R* applied). Accordingly even if the happenings at Whiddy could properly be regarded as confined to the vessel itself, the Irish courts would still have jurisdiction to try the issues involved. The wish of the first named defendants to have the matter tried in Ireland and the fact that had the plaintiffs not joined the third named defendants the first named defendants would have applied to issue third party proceedings against them weighed heavily in favour of having the matter tried in Ireland. The overriding factor was whether the defendants were liable to the plaintiffs under the law of tort in Ireland, and in the circumstances the application would be refused.

Cases referred to in judgment
Chung Chi Cheung v R [1938] 4 All ER 786
Cripps Warburg v Cologne Investment Co Ltd, Aran Friendly Society and Others [1980] IR 321
Freedman v Opdeheyde (1945) Ir Jur Rep 22
In re Kernot (An Infant) Kernot v Tiernal [1965] 1 Ch D 217
Sayers v International Drilling Co NV [1971] 3 All ER 163

Reported at [1983] ILRM 163

LABOUR LAW

IBM Ireland Ltd v John Feeney: Circuit Court 1982 No. 8 (Judge Ryan) 11 May 1982.

Employer and Employee - Unfair dismissal - Initiation of claim - Time limit - Whether mandatory requirement on employee to notify employer - Unfair Dismissals Act, 1977, *(No. 10) s. 8.*

Facts S. 8 (2) of the Unfair Dismissals Act, 1977, insofar as it is relevant, is in the terms following: 'A claim for redress . . . shall be initiated by giving a notice in writing . . . to a rights commissioner or the tribunal, as the case may be, within 6 months of the date of the relevant dismissal and a copy of the notice shall be given to the employer concerned within the same period'. The respondent had brought a claim for compensation before the Employment Appeals Tribunal, pursuant to the terms of the Act of 1977 against his former employer who was the appellant in the instant case. Counsel for the employer had sought the ruling of the tribunal as to whether or not, having regard to the provisions of s. 8 (2) of the Act, the claimant's claim was time barred as his claim, though served on the tribunal within six months of the date of the dismissal, was not served on the employer within the said six months period. The tribunal had ruled that the word 'shall' when used in the clause pertaining to service of the notice on the tribunal was mandatory, whereas the use of the word 'shall' in the clause pertaining to service of the copy notice on the employer was regulatory only. From this ruling the employer appealed to the Circuit Court.

Held In allowing the appeal, that the second part of s. 8(2) is a mandatory requirement which obliges the employee to serve the necessary notice on the employer within the 6 months period.

Cases referred to in judgment
Howard v Bodington (1877) 2 PD 203
Liverpool Borough Bank v Turner 29 LJ (Ch) 827

Reported at [1983] ILRM 50

Stanley R. Lewis v Squash Ireland Ltd: Employment Appeals Tribunal 1982 No. M250/UD146/82 (Donal Hamilton [Chairman], Arthur Rice and George Keenan) 14 February 1983

Employer and Employee - Unfair dismissal - Contract of employment tainted with illegality - Whether illegal aspect severable - Consequence of illegality - Whether contract void or unenforceable - Unfair Dismissals Act, 1977 (No. 10)

Facts The appellant claimed compensation for his dismissal by the respondent company. He had been employed as managing director of the company. The issue of whether the dismissal was unfair was the subject of evidence over thirteen days. His salary was £16,000 per annum, part of which, £2,000, was treated in the respondent company's books as an expense. It had been agreed between the parties that this payment was a salary increase. The Tribunal expressed the view that the non-inclusion of the £2,000 in the appellant's remuneration was contrary to his obligation to account fully under the PAYE system. Counsel were invited to make submissions on whether the contract was tainted with illegality, and if so, the effect on the appellant's claim.

Determination The payment of £2,000 made to the appellant was part of his remuneration and was misdescribed as an expense. The scheme adopted in relation to its payment was illegal and amounted to a fraud on the revenue.

The Tribunal rejected a submission by counsel for the appellant that the illegal term could be severed from the remainder of the contract of employment. The term had been incorporated by the consent of both parties. The illegality did not render the contract void, but unenforceable at the suit of the appellant; public policy is set against such enforcement.

In order that an employee be able to have his claim dealt with under the Unfair

Dismissals Act 1977, he must be an 'employee' at law.
Both of the appellant's claims were dismissed.

Cases referred to in determination
Black v Grealy High Court 1977 No. 4004P (Costello J) 10 November 1977
Corby v Morrison [1980] ICR 564 EAT
Coral Leisure Group Ltd v Barnett [1981] ICR 503
Davidson v Pillay (1979) IRLR 275 EAT
Miller v Karlinski (1945) 62 TLR 85 CA
Newland v Simons v Willer (Hairdressers) Ltd. [1981] ICR 521 EAT
Shaw v Groom [1970] 2QB 504
St. John Shipping Corporation v Joseph Rank Ltd [1957] 1QB 267
Tomlinson v Dick Evans 'U' Drive Ltd. [1978] ICR 639 EAT
Whitecross Potatoes (International) Ltd v R. Coyle High Court 1976 No. 3761P (Finlay P) 23 February 1978.

Peter Shanley SC and Aengus O'Brolchain **for the claimant**
Eoin Fitzsimons SC and Peter Kelly **for the respondent**

Reported at [1983] ILRM 363   [This case is under appeal]

LANDLORD & TENANT

Michael Enock and Leon Hairstylist Ltd v Lambert Jones Estates Ltd and Sydney Vard Ltd: High Court 1982 No. 7248P (Costello J) 30 July 1982.

Landlord and tenant - Forfeiture by landlord - Claim by 'under-lessee' for relief - Person 'claiming as under-lessee' having unenforceable agreement with tenant for a sub-lease - Whether claim maintainable - Conveyancing Act 1892, (No. 10) ss. 4 and 5 - Landlord and Tenant (Amendment) Act 1980, (No. 10) s. 78.

Facts The plaintiffs had leased certain premises to the first defendant. The second defendant had moved into occupation of part of the premises under an agreement with the first defendant for a sub-lease which was conditional on the giving of consent by the plaintiffs. The head-lease contained a prohibition against sub-letting without consent and both defendants knew of this. The first defendant failed to pay rent under the head-lease and the plaintiffs brought an action for possession against both defendants and also claimed an injunction to restrain the second defendant from entering, occupying or being on the premises. The plaintiffs brought a motion for judgment in default of defence against both defendants and a motion for an interlocutory injunction against the second defendant. A decree for possession was made against the first defendant which did not seek to defend the action. The second defendant was given an extension of time to file a defence claiming relief as sub-lessee under s. 4 of the 1892 Act and rights as an 'inferior lessee' under s. 70 of the 1980 Act. The second defendant resisted the motion for the interlocutory injunction on the balance of convenience and on the strength of the defence. S. 9 of the 1892 Act provides that 'under-lease' in the Act 'includes an agreement for an underlease where the under-lessee has become entitled to have his underlease granted'. Counsel for the second defendant claimed that the agreement in this case came within this definition and that an agreement for a lease was as good as a lease under s. 78 of the 1980 Act. Counsel for the plaintiffs argued that the second defendant could not have any rights as 'under-lessee' or 'inferior lessee' and that the balance of convenience favoured the plaintiff.

Held The second defendants did not have an enforceable agreement for a sublease therefore the defence under the 1892 Act did not appear to have much prospect of success at the trial of the action. The claim as 'inferior lessee' under s. 78 of the 1980 Act could not succeed, even if s. 78 covered a person in occupation under an agreement for a lease, because s. 78 could not be interpreted as granting rights to a person in occupation under an unenforceable agreement. At the hearing it was probable that the second defendant would be ordered to leave the premises. The plaintiffs were entitled to an interlocutory injunction because the plaintiffs would suffer a greater loss if wrongfully refused possession than the loss the defendant would suffer if wrongfully ordered to leave. Furthermore the defendant would be able to find comparable premises to trade from, whereas the plaintiffs would not be able to let the premises as a single unit if refused possession. The interlocutory injunction was therefore granted.

No cases referred to in judgment

[This case has been appealed to the Supreme Court]
Reported at [1983] ILRM 532

LICENSING

The Director of Public Prosecutions v Vincent O'Toole: High Court 1982 No. 63 SS (Finlay P) 17 May 1982.

Licensing - Liquor licence - Licensing offences - Selling etc. liquor during prohibited hours - Conviction - Substantial meal supplied and eaten with the drinks remaining not fully consumed - Whether liquor 'being consumed' at the time same - Intoxicating Liquor Act, 1927, (No. 15) s. 13 - Intoxicating Liquor Act, 1960, (No. 18) s.5 - Intoxicating Liquor Act, 1962, (No. 21) s. 4.

Facts The defendant was licensee of premises known as The Maryland Hotel situated in the City of Waterford. At 12.05 a.m. on 11 April, 1981 members of the Garda Siochana found on the premises ten people consisting of six seated together at a table, and four seated together at the bar counter. All ten people had earlier consumed a substantial meal served after 11 p.m., and at the time of entry of the Gardai all ten people were drinking intoxicating liquor. The defendant was charged with and found guilty of offences contrary to the provisions of s. 13 of the Intoxicating Liquor Act, 1927 as inserted by s. 5 of the Intoxicating Liquor Act, 1960 as amended by s. 4 of the Intoxicating Liquor Act, 1962.

The facts as stated constituted an offence unless the defendant could bring himself within the exemption contained in s. 13 of the Act of 1927 and inserted by s. 5 of the Act of 1960. The material provisions of the exemptions are that 'In each case the intoxicating liquor is (i) ordered by that person at the same time as a substantial meal is ordered by him, (ii) consumed at the same time as and with the meal, (iii) supplied and consumed in the portion of the premises usually set apart for the supply of meals, (iv) paid for at the same time as the meal is paid for'. The District Justice concluded that the defendant had failed to come within the exemptions numbered at (i) (ii) and (iv) and convicted accordingly. The defendant appealed by way of a case stated.

Held The District Justice had erred in law in holding that the defendant had failed to prove himself within the exemptions stipulated in s. 13 of the Intoxicating Liquor Act, 1927 as amended.
1. Following the construction of exemption (ii) above as outlined in the decision of *The Attorney General (Doherty) v Gilsenan*, the alcohol being consumed at 12.05 a.m. could properly be described as being consumed at the same time as and with the meal notwithstanding the fact that the eating of the meal had finished before that time.
2. As regards exemption (iv), on a reasonable interpretation of the subsection the drinks being consumed could properly be said to have been paid for at the same time as the meal was being paid for; the same span of time rather than the same precise moment being the proper construction thereof.

Case referred to in judgment
The Attorney General (Doherty) v Gilsenan High Court 1960 No.   (Davitt P) 5 July 1963.

Reported at [1983] ILRM 41

NATURAL JUSTICE

The State (Williams) v The Army Pensions Board and The Minister for Defence: Supreme Court 1981 No. 33 (Henchy J, Hederman and McCarthy JJ) 14 February 1983.

Defence Forces - Army Pensions Board - Application for widow's allowance rejected - Denial of oral hearing - Refusal to furnish evidence on which decision based - Whether breach of natural justice - Nature of Board - Whether judicial or administrative - Whether Board's power to grant allowance enabling or mandatory - Army Pensions Act 1962 (No. 22) Second Schedule - Army Pensions Act 1968, (No. 12) s. 11(1)(c) - Army Pensions (Investigation of Applications) Regulations 1927, regs 8, 10- (SI No. 6 of 1928)

Facts The applicant's late husband had served in the Army from 1939 until his death in 1978 when his widow, the applicant, applied to the Army Pensions

Board for certain allowances and gratuities specified in the Second Schedule to the Army Pensions Act, 1962. The Board refused the application. All of the medical records were in the possession of the Army Medical Authorities. The records were made available to the Board, but Mrs Williams' requests that the records be examined on her behalf were turned down. Art. 10 of the relevant Regulations (SI No. 6 of 1928) empowers the Board to reconsider the application in the light of any additional evidence which an applicant might submit. Mrs Williams made such an application, but as she was unable to submit any further evidence the Board again disallowed her claim on the grounds that no additional evidence had been received on her behalf. In the High Court the application for a conditional order of certiorari quashing two reports of the Army Pensions Board was refused.

Held (Henchy and McCarthy JJ, Hederman J concurring), In allowing the appeal, that the Board had acted in breach of natural justice: the applicant had been unfairly and unjustly prevented from rebutting the initial conclusions reached by the Board.

Cases referred to in judgment
Application of Dunne [1968] IR 105 citing *McDougall v Paterson* 11 CB 755
Kiely v The Minister for Social Welfare [1977] IR 267
Williams v Army Pensions Board, The Minister for Defence Ireland and the Attorney General [1981] ILRM 379

Reported at [1983] ILRM 331

The State (At the Prosecution of Brian Hussey, Henry B. Sisk and Donal Chambers) v Irish The Land Commission, Michael Cleary and Michael B. O'Cleary: High Court 1982 No. 542 SS (Hamilton J) 20 October 1982.

Land Commission - Acquisition of Lands - Objectors application for sight of certain documents refused - Whether procedure adopted fair and in accordance with principles of natural justice - Land Act 1965 (No. 2) ss. 12, 45.

Facts On the hearing of the prosecutor's objections before the second and third named respondent Lay Commissioners to the acquisition of certain lands by the first named respondent, it was contended by the prosecutors that the Land Commission were not acting *bona fide* in their dealings with the prosecutors. The second named respondent directed that the tribunal be furnished with particulars of all transactions between the first named prosecutor and his associates and associate companies and this direction was complied with by the prosecutors. However the Land Commission were only prepared to make available to the prosecutors the files relating to the land the subject matter of the objections. The prosecutors applied to the second named respondent for an order directing the Land Commission to furnish other documents but the prosecutors application was refused. The prosecutors applied for and got a conditional order of certiorari against such refusal and now applied to have the order made absolute.

Held by Hamilton J in making the conditional order absolute. The principles of natural justice imposed a clear and positive obligation on the second and third named respondents to adopt procedures which were fair and having indicated to the prosecutor that they would direct production of the documents concerned it was wrong of the second and third named respondents not to impose a similar obligation on the Land Commission to that which they indicated they would impose on the prosecutors. *Kiely v Minister of Social Welfare* [1977] IR 267 and *Nolan v Irish Land Commission* [1981] IR 20.

Cases referred to in judgment
In re Haughey [1971] IR 217
Kiely v The Minister for Social Welfare [1977] IR 267
Nolan v The Irish Land Commission [1981] IR 23

Reported at [1983] ILRM 407

NEGLIGENCE

Cole (An Infant) v Webb Caravans Ltd and Roadmaster Ireland Ltd:
High Court (Cork Circuit) 1980 No. 4300P (Keane J) 20 October 1983.

Negligence - Product liability - Liability of supplier - Onus of proof.

Facts The plaintiff claimed damages for negligence and breach of duty against the supplier and, secondly, the manufacturer of a caravan. The plaintiff's case showed that the caravan sold to her father by the first named defendant was defective in that the catch for the door did not work. There was no evidence as to whether the defect was caused in the manufacture or in the subsequent treatment of the caravan, or as to whether there had been any intermediate inspection of the caravan for defects.

At the close of the plaintiff's case, there was an application for the first named defendant to have the case withdrawn from the jury on the grounds:
(1) That there was no evidence to go to the jury upon which the jury might find negligence on the part of the first named defendant and
(2) That as a matter of law, once the supplier of goods has bought them from a reputable manufacturer, there is no duty in tort to the ultimate consumer.

Held Once a plaintiff has adduced evidence which shows that a thing is supplied in a potentially dangerous state, there is a case for the supplier to answer.

Case referred to in judgment
O'Sullivan v Noonan and Transit Ltd Supreme Court 1970 No. 89/103/109, 28 July 1972.

Editor's Note
An account of *O'Sullivan v Noonan and Transit Ltd* may be seen in McMahon & Binchy's *Casebook on the Law of Torts* at page 323.

Reported at [1983] ILRM 595

PATENTS

In the Matter of the Patents Act, 1964; Beecham Group Ltd v Bristol Myers Company: Supreme Court 1981 No. 208 (O'Higgins CJ, Walsh, Henchy, Griffin and Hamilton JJ) 15 February 1983 (Nem. Diss.)

Supreme Court - Patent appeal - Decision of controller - Appeal to the High Court - Whether further appeal to the Supreme Court - Patents Act 1964 (No. 12) ss. 15, 75(7).

Facts The appellants sought to appeal to the Supreme Court from a decision of the High Court on appeal to it under s. 19 of the Patents Act, 1964. S. 75 sub-s. 1 of this Act provides *inter alia* that any appeal from the Controller of Industrial and Commercial Property should be to the High Court and s. 75 permits such appeal on a specified question of law from such decisions of the High Court other than under certain specified sections of the Act, including s. 19. The sections specified all related to powers of the Controller to decide matters arising upon a patent application. The Controller was also given powers elsewhere in the Act to decide matters in relation to patents already granted. The respondents sought by motion to have the appellants' appeal to the Supreme Court struck out as not entertainable, contending that s. 75 sub-s. 7 excluded from the jurisdiction of the Supreme Court decisions on all patents applications save only decisions under s. 15. The appellants contended that an appeal lay in every case, but only upon a question of law save in the specified sections where an appeal was open on all issues of law and fact.

Held If the appellant's contention was correct two types of appeal to the Supreme Court would exist in patent cases: (i) appeals involving all issues of law and facts and (ii) appeals confined to a specified question of law. No basis for this distinction was suggested and such an interpretation would produce a lack of uniformity in patents decisions. The object of s. 75 was the achievement of such uniformity. Accordingly the respondents' interpretation was correct and decisions of the High Court under the sections specified in s. 75 may not be further appealed. Motion allowed.

No cases referred to in judgment

Reported at [1983] ILRM 500

PLANNING

Crodaun Homes Ltd v Kildare County Council: Supreme Court 1981 No. 47 (O'Higgins CJ, Griffin and Hederman JJ) 27 April 1982.

Town and Country Planning - Notice of intention to make application for planning permission - Advertisement in national daily newspaper - Whether compliance with regulations - Whether adequate description of the location of the land - Local Government (Planning & Development) Regulations 1977 (SI No. 65) Arts 14, 15.

Facts Art. 14 of the Planning Regulations 1977 provides that an applicant shall publish notice of his intention to make a planning application in a newspaper circulating in the district in which the relevant land is situate. Art. 15 provides that the notice must contain the location of the land or the address of the structure to which the application relates. The plaintiffs sought planning permission for a development which they described in a newspaper notice as 'Co. Kildare Full permission sought for 14 bungalows at Leixlip Gate Crodaun Homes Limited'. At the expiration of two months from the defendants acknowledgement of the application the plaintiffs sought permission pursuant to s.26(4) Local Government (Planning and Development) Act, 1963 by reason of the defendants failure to notify their decision within this period. The defendants contended that the notice did not state the location of the lands sought to be developed as required by the 1977 regulations and that the public were not given the notice to which they were entitled. The plaintiffs obtained an order of the High Court declaring that they had secured planning permission and the defendants appealed.

Held By Griffin J (Hederman J concurring) The letter and the spirit of the 1977 regulations required that in the case of land, and in particular land which is not in an urban area, the site on which it is proposed that the development should take place must be accurately so described in relation to the district in which the land is situate as to be readily and reasonably identifiable. In omitting the word 'Celbridge' from the description of the lands in the notice, the notice given to the public was incomplete and inadequate. The application did not, therefore, comply with Arts. 14 and 15 and accordingly no question of planning permission by default could arise. Appeal allowed.

Per O'Higgins CJ: (Dissenting) The object of the 1977 regulations is to ensure that the location of the site to be developed is to be known in particular to people in the locality, and on the evidence the notice might have contained a far more accurate description than the alternatives suggested.

No cases referred to in judgment.

Reported at [1983] ILRM 1

The State (Genport Ltd) v An Bord Pleanala: High Court 1981 No. 523 SS (Finlay P) 1 February 1982.

Town and Country Planning - Extension erected without planning permission - Permission to retain refused by planning authority - Appeal to Bord - Whether appeal valid - Natural justice - Local Government (Planning & Development) Act 1976 (No. 20) s. 17, 18 - Local Government (Planning & Development) Regulations 1977 (SI No. 65) r. 35.

Facts The prosecutor's architects, by a letter which omitted the grounds of appeal, appealed to the respondent against a refusal of planning permission. The Board, in a letter dated 14 July 1981 warned the architects that the appeal would be determined if within 14 days the grounds of appeal were not submitted. Before rejecting the appeal on 4 November 1981 the Board sent to the architects notifications of objections inviting comments thereon. The Board also acknowledged, without objection, a letter of 6 August 1981 from the architects indicating that they were delaying submission of grounds of appeal.

Held The letter of 14 July 1981 complied with s. 18 of the Act of 1976 and the notification of objections complied with s. 17 of the Act. However the reply to the letter of 6 August 1981 coupled with the subsequent notifications of objections could be construed as a waiver by the Board of its right after expiry of the 14 days to determine the appeal without further notice. Because of the possibility of an injustice the decision of the Board should be quashed.

Case referred to in judgment.
The State (Elm Developments) v An Bord Pleanala [1981] ILRM 108.

Reported at [1983] ILRM 12

The Right Honourable The Lord Mayor Aldermen and Burgesses of Dublin v Maiden Poster Sites Ltd.: High Court 1982 No. 38 MCA (Murphy J) 8 July 1982.

Town and Country Planning - Application for order restraining continued unauthorised development - Works representing considerable improvement to the appearance of the premises - Subsequent application for permission to retain refused - Appeal to An Bord Pleanala - Whether court power to direct removal - Whether pending appeal inhibits the granting of an injunction - Local Government (Planning and Development) Act 1976, (No. 20) s. 27.

Facts The respondents erected four advertising hoardings on premises they had acquired for that purpose. An application was subsequently made for planning permission which was refused, and the appeal before An Bord Pleanala was pending when the applicants sought an order restraining the respondents' use of a continued unauthorised development. The respondents submitted that the advertising hoarding, although unauthorised, had enhanced the appearance and amenities of premises which has become delapidated.

Held by Murphy J in granting the application. That the court should not facilitate the respondent from deriving an income from an unauthorised development.

Case referred to in judgment
Morris v Garvey [1982] ILRM 177

Reported at [1983] ILRM 48

The State (Flynn & O'Flaherty Ltd) v The Lord Mayor Aldermen and Burgesses of the City of Dublin: High Court 1982 No 71SS (Murphy J), 30 April 1982.

Certiorari - Conditional order not served in time - Application for extension of the time for service - Whether order automatically discharged - statutory time limit for challenging decision of An Bord Pleanala having expired - Local Government (Planning and Development) Act 1963 (No. 28) s. 82 (3A) - RSC Order 108 Rule 7.

Facts The respondents made an order on 22 December 1981, refusing planning permission to the applicants to develop certain premises named in the application. The applicants obtained a conditional order of certiorari against the respondents on the 22 December 1981. The order directed that the order should be served within ten days of the date thereof and provided that cause should be shown within twenty-one days of service of the order. The conditional order of certiorari was not served until 2 April 1982 and it was received by the respondents on 6 April 1982. The applicants applied for an order extending the time for service.

Held By Murphy J 1. That the court had no jurisdiction to grant an extension of time.
2. A conditional order of certiorari is automatically discharged if it is not served within the time specified by the rule, or within any time fixed by the court at the time of its making or by way of further order before it has been automatically discharged providing that there are no existing or substantive proceedings capable of being extended.

Case referred to in judgment
The State (Raymond Fitzsimons) v District Justice Donal Kearney High Court 1978 No. 415SS (Finlay P) 25 May 1979.

Reported at [1983] ILRM 125

Thomas Gerard O'Neill v Clare County Council: High Court 1979 No. 2564P (McWilliam J) 18 May 1982.

Town and Country Planning - Effective date of application - Whether failure to adjudicate on and give notice of decision within prescribed period - Entitlement to damages - Assessment of damages - Local Government (Planning and Development) Act 1963, (No. 28) s. 26(4) (5).

Facts The plaintiff applied to the defendant for planning permission for 18 houses. Subsequently he gave particulars of the proposed public lighting and excluded one site from the application. The defendant made no decision within 2 months, and approximately $3\frac{1}{2}$ months after the application the defendant purported to notify the plaintiff of a decision to grant permission with conditions. The plaintiff objected to this. 9 months after the application the defendant granted permission (without conditions). The plaintiff brought this action seeking a declaration that by virtue of s. 26 of the Act a decision to grant permission should be regarded as having been given 2 months after the application and that the purported notification of a decision to grant permission with conditions was void. The plaintiff also sought damages for the delay.

Held The furnishing, subsequent to the application of the particulars and the exclusion of one site did not constitute a new application postponing the running of the 2 month period. The plaintiff was entitled to the declarations sought and to damages for the delay in granting permission as the defendant had been guilty of a default which for part of the time had been deliberate.

Case referred to in judgment
Frank Dunne Ltd v Dublin Corporation [1974] IR 45.

Cases referred to in legal argument
Kenny v Cosgrove [1926] IR 517
Phillips v.Britannia Hygienic Laundry Ltd [1923] 2 KB 832.
The State (Abenglen Properties Ltd) v Dublin Corporation [1982] ILRM 590.
The State (Pine Valley Development Ltd) v Dublin County Council [1982] ILRM 169.

Reported at [1983] ILRM 141

The State (Magauran) v Dublin Corporation: Supreme Court 1979 No 177 (Henchy, J, Griffin and Hederman JJ) 22 July 1982 (Nem. Diss.)

Town and Country Planning - Application for permission for change of use - Default permission - Housing authority requiring particulars as to whether premises were remaining primarily residential - Whether applicant obliged to furnish particulars - Local Government (Planning and Development) Act, 1963 (No. 28) s. 26(4) - Housing Act, 1969 (No. 16) ss 1(1), 2(1), 2(2), 3, 9(2), 10(c).

Facts The prosecutor sought planning permission from the respondent to obtain change of use of one room of a dwellinghouse to office use. In his application for planning permission the prosecutor stated that his submission did not require Housing Act permission because the house was principally used as a dwelling and the change did not cause a change of residence on the part of a person who was ordinarily resident in the house. The Corporation in reply to the application stated that the proposed development required a separate permission under the Housing Act of 1969 and then requested an answer to certain particulars listed in their replying letter. The prosecutor refused to furnish the particulars requested and then applied successfully for a conditional order of mandamus directing the corporation as the relevant planning authority to grant him the required planning permission. When the respondents showed cause the conditional order was made absolute and the trial judge held that the planning permission had accrued by default to the prosecutor, under s. 26(4) of the Local Government (Planning and Development) Act, 1963. The respondents appealed.

Held by Henchy J in allowing the appeal against the grant of an absolute order of mandamus and in discharging the conditional order:
(i) The planning authority has a statutory entitlement to demand certain prerequisites from an applicant. Until such prerequisites are satisfied, or ruled applicable, a development permission cannot be validly granted, either expressly or by default under s. 26(4) of the 1963 Act.
(ii) It is for the applicant to prove the existence of the exemption, and the adjudication has to be made in the first instance by the relevant Housing Authority.

No cases referred to in judgment

Reported at [1983] ILRM 145

Ignatius Byrne v Dublin County Council: High Court 1982 No. 75SS (Gannon J) 29 July 1982

Local Government - Planning and Development - Application for outline planning permission refused - Application for compensation - extent to which value of land reduced - Alternative potential development - Planning authority undertaking to grant permission for an alternative development - Whether authority power to give such an undertaking - Whether such undertaking valid - Local Government (Planning and Development) Act 1963, (No. 28) ss. 55, 57.

Facts S. 55 of the Local Government (Planning and Development) Act 1963 as amended provides *inter alia* in sub. s. (1) that if on a claim made to the planning authority it is shown that as a result of a decision under part IV of the Act involving a refusal of permission to develop land the value of an interest of any person existing in the land to which the decision relates at the time of the decision is reduced such person shall be entitled to be paid by way of compensation the amount of such reduction in value. Subs. (2) provides that *inter alia* in determining reduction of value for the purpose of this section regard shall be had ... (b) to any undertaking that may be given to grant permission to develop the land in the event of application being made under this Act in that behalf and (c) to the fact that exempted development may be carried out on the land. S.57 of the 1963 Act provides *inter alia* that where a claim for compensation under this part of the Act is made in respect of an interest in land permission for the development ... shall be taken ... to be available with respect to that land ... if there is in force with respect to that land ... a grant of or an undertaking to grant permission under this Act for some such development. The claimant owner and farmer of 65 acres of agricultural land at the northern part of the Portmarnock peninsula in County Dublin unsuccessfully applied for Outline Planning Permission for a proposed housing development and car park on these lands and subsequently applied for compensation under s. 55. His claim was referred to an arbitrator nominated by the Land Values Reference Committee. During the course of the hearing before the arbitrator the respondant planning authority produced an undertaking which purported to be an undertaking to grant permission for a development to which s. 57 of the 1963 Act applied. The arbitrator by special case stated requested the opinion of the High Court as to (a) whether the respondents had power to issue a valid undertaking to grant a planning premission in accordance with s. 57, (b) if not whether s. 57 precluded the arbitrator from awarding compensation under s. 55 having regard to the undertaking given during the hearing, (c)(i) if so whether the undertaking was valid within the meaning of s. 57 (ii) whether it was in force (iii) whether it was given in time to preclude any award of compensation and (d) whether it was an undertaking within the meaning of s. 55 of the 1963 Act. The claimant contended that there could be no such thing as an undertaking to invoke s. 57 since for it to be in force it had to have been (a) in existence at the same time as the grant of permission for which it would provide an alternative (b) preceded by a decision taken in accordance with prescribed procedures (c) such as to specify *inter alia* the land to which it related and (d) capable of being acted upon.

Held The function of the court when presented with statutory requirements was to accept them and insofar as possible to give them effect in a sensible manner in accordance with the manifest intention of the statute as shown by its provisions. S. 57 did not arise until a claim for compensation under s. 55 had been made. It was not intended that the undertaking to grant permission was to be equated to grant of permission and s. 57 could be construed despite the demonstrated weakness of expression as precluding an award of compensation to a claimant such as in this case who had land capable of being developed in a manner indicated in s. 57 if the planning authority expressly stated that it undertook that it would grant permission for some such development. Accordingly, the respondant had power to give a valid undertaking in accordance with s. 57, the undertaking given in the instant case was valid within s. 57, was in force, and was given in time to preclude the award of compensation under s. 55.

Case referred to in judgment
Owenabue Ltd v Dublin County Council [1982] ILRM 150

Reported at [1983] ILRM 213

Carrick Hall Holdings Ltd v Dublin Corporation: High Court 1979 No. 406SP (McWilliam J) 30 June 1982

Local Government - Planning and Development - Hotel premises - Hotel acquiring ordinary seven day licence - Ground floor reconstructed to incorporate a lounge bar - Increase in trade - Whether material change of use constituting development - Whether, if so, such development exempted development - Local Government (Planning and Development) Act 1963, (No. 28) s. 5 - Housing Act 1969, (No. 16) s. 10

Facts The plaintiff purchased in 1975 a hotel in Orwell Road, Dublin with a hotel licence. The plaintiff then obtained an ordinary seven day licence, and having converted part of the ground floor of the premises into a lounge bar carried on an ordinary publican's lounge bar trade. These changes led to a large increase in the licensed trade, in the number of cars travelling on and parked on Orwell Road, frequently blocking the gateways of the residents; to a considerable increase in noise in the late evenings; and to a certain amount of abuse by customers of residents.

An Bord Pleanala, on a reference to it by the defendant under s. 5 of the 1963 Act, decided that the change of use of the premises from use as a hotel without a public bar to use as a hotel with a public bar was development within the meaning of the 1963 Act, and was not exempted development. The plaintiff appealed to the High Court against this decision. The plaintiff argued that as a licensed trade had been carried on before the construction of the public bar there had been no change of use.

Held Intensification of use can be a material change of use. An increase in vehicular traffic is relevant in deciding if there has been a material change of use. In this case the evidence was conclusive that the change from a hotel licence without a public bar to an ordinary seven day licence with a public bar had changed the whole character of the business carried on and had caused the increase in traffic, parking, noise and other unsatisfactory changes in amenities for the local residents. There were ample grounds for the decision of An Bord Pleanala. Appeal dismissed.

Cases referred to in judgment
Brooks and Burton Ltd v Environment Secretary [1977] 1 WLR 1294

Hamilton and anor v West Sussex County Council [1958] 2 QB 286
Jennings Motors Ltd v Environment Secretary [1982] 2 WLR 131
Patterson v Murphy High Court 1977 No. 6215P (Costello J) 4 May 1978.
Readymix (Eire) Ltd v Dublin County Council Supreme Court 30 July 1974

Reported at [1983] ILRM 268 [This case is under Appeal]

Creedon v Dublin Corporation: Supreme Court 1978 No. 267 (O'Higgins CJ, Hederman and McCarthy JJ) 11 February 1983 *(nem. diss.)*

Local Government - Housing Authority - Application for permission to use premises other than for human habitation refused - Whether such decision invalid - Default procedure - Whether operative -Local Government (Planning & Development) Act, 1963 (No. 28), ss. 2, 26 - Housing Act, 1969 (No. 16) ss. 4, 10.

Facts The plaintiff sought permission from the defendant, the housing authority, for permission under s. 4 of the Housing Act, 1969 to use certain premises other than for human habitation. An application for planning permission under the Local Government (Planning and Development) Act 1963, had already been lodged by the plaintiff before the housing application, but this had been postponed by agreement. The housing application was refused by the defendant on the grounds that such a change would result in a reduction in the supply of housing in the functional area of Dublin Corporation. The plaintiff then commenced proceedings by way of plenary summons, seeking, a declaration (i) that the decision of the corporation was in conflict with the facts of the application and that it was both unreasonable and contrary to natural justice, and that as a consequence, (ii) the order was a nullity and that pursuant to the Housing Act 1969 s. 4, the court should deem permission to have been granted to the plaintiff after the lapse of the appropriate period of five weeks during which no valid decision had been made by the corporation. In the High Court the plaintiff's claim was dismissed.

Held by the Supreme Court in dismissing the plaintiff's appeal:
1. The function of the court, while discretionary, cannot be used in abbeting attempts at side-stepping the legislative and administrative procedures by recourse to the courts.
2. The decision of the Housing Authority was invalid, as the defendant had misconstrued the law.
3. The plaintiff, however, was not entitled to a declaration that the planning permission was deemed to have been granted since he had not exhausted the statutory remedies available, in that he had failed to pursue the right of appeal to the Minister as provided by s. 4(6) of the 1969 Act.

Cases referred to in judgment
The State (Abenglen Properties Ltd) v Dublin Corporation [1982] ILRM 590
Listowel Urban District Council v McDonagh [1968] IR 312
Reported at [1983] ILRM 339

Dublin County Council v Nora Teresa Shortt: Supreme Court 1982
No. 18 (O'Higgins CJ, Henchy and Hederman JJ) 13 May 1983 (Nem. Diss.)

Local Government - Compulsory Acquisition - Valuation - Subject land designated on the County Dublin Development Plan - Whether designation amounts to a reservation for a particular purpose - Whether, in the event of housing development taking place, sanitary authority would refuse a connection for sewerage - Public Health (Ireland) Act 1878, (Ch. 25) s. 23 - Acquisition of Land (Assessment of Compensation) Act 1919, (Ch. 57) s. 2 - Local Government (Planning and Development) Act 1963, (No. 28) ss. 55, 56(1)(b)(i), 69, 4th Schedule Rule 11

Facts The County Council had acquired by compulsory purchase order certain lands in County Dublin, the property of the respondent. In the course of arbitration proceedings the arbitrator referred four questions by way of case stated to the High Court. The first two questions were as follows:
Whether the designation accorded to the subject lands amounted to a reservation for a particular purpose within the statutory rules for the assessment of compensation. Rule 11 is one of the Rules contained in the fourth schedule to the Local Government (Planning and Development) Act, 1963 and inserted into s. 2 of the Acquisition of Land (Assessment of Compensation) Act, 1919 by s. 69 of the 1963 Act. It provides as follows in relation to the assessment of compensation:

> (11) Regard shall not be had to any depreciation or increase in value attributable to —
> (a) the land, or any land in the vicinity thereof, being reserved for any particular purpose in a development plan, or (b) inclusion of the land in a special amenity area order.

(3) Whether the County Council as sanitary authority could in the event of housing development taking place on the subject lands, refuse a connection for sewerage to its main sewer.
(4) In the event of such development being proposed could the County Council refuse permission under the provisions of s. 56 sub-s. 1(b)(i) of the Planning Act 1963 on the basis that it was premature in that there was an existing deficiency in the provision of water supply or sewerage facilities.
If a refusal is properly made on such grounds, compensation under the provisions of s. 55 is not payable. In the High Court all questions were answered in the affirmative by McMahon J [1982] ILRM 117. The County Council appealed.

Held by O'Higgins CJ, (Henchy and Hederman JJ concurring) in dismissing the appeal and affirming the judgment of McMahon J
2. In answer to question one and two, Rule 11 refers to land set apart from other land in the area and is zoned for a different purpose and in valuing such land the arbitrator is to value the land having regard to the purpose for which the land generally in the area is zoned.
3. In answering question three in the negative, s. 23 of the Public Health (Ireland) Act 1873, is not repealed by implication by the provisions of the 1963 Act.

4. The reply to question four is in the affirmative because such a decision would not be within the provisions of s. 56 (1) (b)(i) of the 1963 Act.

No cases referred to in judgment

Reported at [1983] ILRM 377

Rosemary Gammell v Dublin County Council: High Court 1978 No. 1547P (Carroll J) 28 January 1983

Local Government - Unlicensed caravan site - All occupants rehoused - County Council prohibiting the erection or retention of any temporary dwellings on the site - Whether order void - Order having no effect until person aggrieved has been given an opportunity of stating reasons as to why it should not come into operation - Whether sufficient compliance with principals of natural justice - Local Government (Sanitary Services) Act 1948, (No. 3) ss. 31(1) (3) (8) (9) (10), 34 - Local Government Act 1955, (No. 9) s. 66

Facts The plaintiff owned a caravan park in Malahide which she had bought in 1974. It has been used as such since 1959. She had been informed that no action would be taken under the Local Government (Planning and Development Act 1963, in relation to the continuation of use. In 1975 the defendant informed her by letter that the site was not licensed as a caravan site as required by s. 34 of the Local Government (Sanitary Services) Act 1948. She did not apply for a licence. In 1977 the persons living in the caravans were re-housed by the defendant. On 12 September 1977 the defendant, as sanitary authority, acting under s. 31(1) of the 1948 Act made an order prohibiting the erection or retention of any temporary dwelling on the caravan site. The order was made because the defendant wanted to ensure no further families to become residents and therefore require re-housing and also for the reason of public health in the area. As required by s. 31(9), notice of the making of this order was published within 14 days after it was made, *i.e.* on 22 September 1977, in a newspaper, the *Irish Press*, circulating in the sanitary district of the defendant. In accordance with s. 31(9) the notice stated that any person aggrieved by the order might within 14 days from the date of publication send to the Minister for the Environment an application in writing for the annulment of the order stating the reasons. No application for the annulment of the order was received within the statutory time limit. On 10 October the defendant wrote to Mrs Gammel telling her that the order prohibiting the erection or retention of temporary dwellings on the site had been made and warning her that if any of the caravan sites were re-occupied, legal proceedings would be taken. This was the first that Mrs Gammell knew of the making of the order. She had no knowledge of any inspection of the site made by certain officials who had certified that the erection or retention of temporary dwellings on the site would be prejudicial to public health and the amenities of the area. On 24 October the notice was published in the *Irish Press* that the said order came into force on 23 October 1977. S. 31(8)(a) provides that an order under the section shall come into force, if no application for its annulment is made, 30 days after a copy of the order is published pursuant to sub-section 9. S. 31(8)(b) provides that if an application is made for the annulment of the order and the order is not annulled thereon, the order shall come into force 14 days after the determination of the application. Under s. 66 of the Local Government Act 1955 an order made under s. 31 may be revoked either by the sanitary authority with the Minister's consent, or by the Minister after consultation with the authority.

The plaintiff brought this action seeking a declaration that the order was void because the requirements of natural justice were not observed in that no notice was given to her prior to the making of the order to enable her to make representations to the defendant. She claimed that the provisions of the section enabling an aggrieved person to apply to the Minister to annul the order did not supply this lack of natural justice.

Held The plaintiff's claim was dismissed. The requirements of the *audi alteram partem* rule had not been breached because representations can be made under s. 31 before the order comes into effect. There is a distinction between cases where an order becomes effective before the person affected has an opportunity to make representations and those cases, such as is the case under s. 31, where machinery provides for an order to be made with delayed effect giving an opportunity to interested parties to make representations for annulment which, if successful, will result in the order never becoming operative. In the first type of case, the requirements of natural justice are breached even though some appellate body may subsequently grant a hearing whereas in the second type of case there is no such breach. *Ingle v O'Brien* (1975) 109 ILTR 7 and *Moran v AG* (1976) 110 ILTR 85 distinguished.

Cases referred to in judgment
The State (Duffy) v The Minister for Defence, Supreme Court 1979 No. 179 9 May 1979
Ingle v O'Brien (1975) 109 ILTR 7
Leary v The National Union of Vehicle Builders [1971] Chan 34
Moran v The Attorney General & Ors. (1976) 110 ILTR 85 (HC)

Reported at [1983] ILRM 413

PRACTICE & PROCEDURE

John Magauran v P M Dargan and P M Dargan and Partner Ltd: High Court 1981 No. 39 MCA (Gannon J) 12 February 1981.

Practice and Procedure - Taxation of Costs - Whether legal costs accountant right of audience before taxing master - Function of taxing master - Whether taxing master exercising a judicial function - Nature of documents - Whether duplication of charge - Solicitors Act 1954 (No. 36) s. 58.

Facts The applicant sought an injunction under s. 27 of the Local Government (Planning and Development) Act, 1976 against the respondents. The application was refused and costs were awarded to the respondents. The payment of the respondents' costs was referred to taxing master de Valera. A hearing was convened by the Taxing Master to review the costs and to hear objections lodged by the applicant. The applicant appeared in person while the respondents were represented by a legal cost accountant only who appeared without either solicitor or counsel attending. The applicant objected to the Taxing Master that only a solicitor or counsel had right of audience before him on taxation of costs. The Taxing Master overruled his objection and proceeded with review of taxation. The applicant sought a high court declatation that the certificate of taxation of Master de Valera was null and void.

Held by Gannon J in dismissing the application.
The Taxing Master does not sit as a court nor does he perform a function in aid of the court. Subject to the requirements of the rules of court governing taxations of costs he has an absolute discretion as to who may attend before him.

Case referred to in judgment
Battle v Irish Art Promotion Centre Ltd [1968] IR 252

Reported at [1983] ILRM 7

Mellowhide Products Ltd v Barry Agencies Ltd: High Court 1981 No. 5615 (Finlay P) 22 February 1982.

Practice - Interest - Monies due and owing for goods supplied and delivered - Matter coming before Master of the High Court - Order plaintiff be at liberty to enter final judgment for amount claimed together with interest - This order being made in default of appearance - Whether within the jurisdiction of the Master to make an order in respect of interest - Meaning of phrase 'judge of the High Court' - Matter coming before High Court for leave to enter judgment - Whether order for interest should be made - Summons not including a claim for interest - Whether relevant - Debtors (Ireland) Act 1840,(Ch. 105)s.26 - Courts Act 1981,(No. 11) ss. 19(1), 22(1)

Facts S. 22 (1) of the Courts Act, 1981 provides that *inter alia* when in any proceedings a court orders the payment of a sum of money the judge concerned may if he thinks fit also order the payment by the person of interest on the whole or any part of the sum. The plaintiff brought summary proceedings to recover £7,747.77 sterling from the defendants and claimed interest pursuant to the courts Act, 1981. The Master of the High Court gave liberty to enter final judgment in default but the registrar of the High Court ruled that she was not satisfied that she had power pursuant to s. 22 to comply with the order of the

Master insofar as it gave leave to enter judgment for interest. On the plaintiff's application, the Master of the High Court discharged his order and transferred the summons to the judge's list.

Held (i) S. 22 (1) could not be construed as giving to the Master of the High Court jurisdiction to make such an order which was strictly confined to judges appointed to the High Court under the Constitution.

(ii) On the facts, interest would be awarded under s. 22 since the plaintiff's claim was between two commercial firms for goods sold and delivered, the defendants had submitted no reasons why in justice they should not pay interest, a debtor delaying due payment of a trading or commercial debt intentionally deprives his creditor of the use of the money concerned, and money could earn higher interest than that which could be awarded under the Act.

(iii) Having regard to the provisions of the Act, it was not necessary to include a claim for interest on the summons.

No cases referred to in judgment

Reported at [1983] ILRM 152

Chemical Bank v Peter McCormack: High Court 1982 No. 9985P (Carroll J) 24 January 1983.

Practice - Bank - Inspection of bank account - Jurisdiction of High Court to make an order for inspection with extra territorial effect - Bankers' Books Evidence Act, 1879 (ch. 11) s. 7 - Bankers' Books Evidence (Amendment) Act, 1959 (No. 21) s.2.

Facts The plaintiffs sued the defendant in respect of a fraud involving $800,000. The plaintiffs alleged that the money was paid into the account of Consumark Incorporated, Bridgeport, USA, and that portion of the money was transferred by the defendant into his personal account with Allied Irish Banks, New York Branch. Subsequently $600,000 was transferred by him by cheque presented to Allied Irish Banks in Dublin drawn upon his New York account. The defendant was sole owner of all the shares in Consumark (Ireland) Ltd. Allied Irish Banks then brought an application to vary an order previously made by Carroll J to discharge so much of the order as gave the plaintiff liberty to inspect and take copies of entries in the books of Allied Irish Banks Ltd at its branch at Park Avenue, New York, USA, and relating to the accounts of Consumark Incorporated and Consumark (Ireland) Ltd at its branches at Dame Street, Dublin and 37/38, O'Connell Street, Dublin. It was submitted on behalf of AIB that the order should be amended as the Irish courts do not have jurisdiction to make an order with extra territorial effect. It was also submitted that the order should be amended by deleting the reference to Consumark Incorporated and Consumark (Ireland) Ltd. on the grounds that notice had not been given to them. The plaintiff submitted that as AIB is a named bank in the definition section by virtue of section 2 of the Bankers' Books Evidence (Amendment) Act 1959, and the subsequent bank mergers, as a named bank all of its branches are included no matter where they are situated.

Held By Carroll J in amending the order:
(i) There are no clear words in the 1879 Act or in the subsequent amending 1959 Act to support the interpretation of an intention to have extra territorial effect. The court does not have jurisdiction to order inspection in a foreign country and therefore the order authorising inspection 'at' the Allied Irish Bank New York Branch is in excess of jurisdiction.
(ii) Although there would appear to be authority for making an order compelling Allied Irish Banks as a company incorporated within the jurisdiction to make available for inspection in this country the accounts of both the defendant and of Consumark Incorporated in the Park Avenue Branch at New York, no such order would be made as it was likely to result in a conflict of jurisdiction and it should also be avoided in the interest of the comity of courts.
(iii) The defendant had been formally notified of the order through his solicitor. As the defendant and Consumark were in reality one and the same, notice would be deemed to be sufficient.

Cases referred to in judgment.
A v C [1982] All ER 347
Attorney General for Alberta v Huggard Assets Ltd [1953] AC 420
Bankers Trust Co. v Shapira & Ors [1980] 3 All ER 353
C.E.B. Draper & Son Ltd v Edward Turner & Son Ltd & Ors [1965] 1 KB 424
Howard v Beale (1889) 23 QBD
R v Grossman (1981) 73 CAR 302
Staunton v Counihan (1957) 92 ILTR 32
Tomalin v S. Pearson & Son Ltd [1909] 2 KB 61

Reported at [1983] ILRM 350   [This case is under appeal]

Catherine Reen v Bank of Ireland Finance Ltd and Luceys Garage (Mallow) Ltd: High Court 1980 No. 9468P (McMahon J) 14 December 1982

Practice - Settlement - Action commenced against two defendants - Plaintiff's counsel entering into settlement agreement with second defendant without adverting to the question of the first defendant's costs - whether unilateral mistake rendering agreement a nullity.

Facts The plaintiff purchased a new motor car on hire purchase terms from the Bank of Ireland. The car was supplied by the second defendant (the motor dealer). The distributors who had been joined as third parties to the action agreed with the dealer to take the defence of the action on behalf of the dealers and negotiations began between the plaintiff's solicitors and the third party's solicitor acting on behalf of the motor dealer. It is alleged to have been given as an inducement to acquire the car on hire purchase. The Bank claimed an indemnity or contribution from the dealers and counterclaimed for arrears of hire purchase instalments against the plaintiff. The distributors who had been joined as third parties agreed with the dealers to take over the defence of the action on behalf of the dealers and negotiations began between the plaintiff's solicitor and the third party's solicitor acting on behalf of the motor dealer. Negotiations were conducted in correspondence and by telephone over a period of months. Subsequently an offer of £3,000 inclusive of costs was made by telephone to the plaintiff's solicitor. The offer was accepted on the same day. Before the settlement cheque for £3,000 was received the plaintiff's solicitor realised that the Bank of Ireland Finance was a party to the action and no provision had been made for payment of the bank's costs. When the case came on for hearing counsel for the motor dealers claimed that the action had been settled. This was disputed by counsel for the plaintiff who argued that it was a case of unilateral mistake on his solicitor's part and that these facts had been known to the defendant's solicitor at the time when the agreement was made and that the agreement was a nullity.

Held By MacMahon J
(i) That the plaintiff's claim had been settled for £3,000 inclusive of costs.
(ii) While there had been a mistake as to the motives for entering into the agreement there had been no mistake as to the terms of the agreement.
(iii) In the absence of any mistake as to the terms of the agreement the third party's solicitor had no duty to enquire if the Bank's costs had been dealt with.

Case referred to in judgment
Smith v Hughes (1871) LR 6QB 597

Reported at [1983] ILRM 507

REVENUE

The Revenue Commissioners v Thomas Finbarr O'Reilly and Patrick McGilligan, Trustees of Club 349: High Court 1981 No. 343R (McWilliam J) 20 May 1982.

Revenue - Exemption from income tax - Club to promote athletic or amateur games or sports - Whether legitimate avoidance of payment of tax - Funds provided by one person - Total control in two trustees - Whether bona fide club - Whether established for sole purpose of 'promoting sport' - Whether two persons can constitute a 'body of persons' - Income Tax Act 1967, (*No. 6*) ss. 1(1), 349.

Facts S. 349 of the Income Tax Act, 1967 provides that exemption shall be granted from income tax in respect of so much of the income of any body of persons established for the sole purpose of promoting athletic or amateur games or sports as is shown to be income which has been or will be applied for that purpose. By s. 1(1) of the Act a body of persons means any body politic corporate or collegiate, and any company, fraternity, fellowship and society of persons whether corporate or not. The defendants were the trustees of Club 349 which was stated to be established for the sole purpose of promoting in particular the sports of snow-skiing, water skiing and sailing. The Appeal Commissioners found *inter alia* that the club was formed after consideration by the defendants of s. 349 of the Act, and that the income of the club arose from interest on loans made to the club by the defendants. The plaintiffs contended that club 349 was not a *bona fide* club, that two persons cannot constitute a body of persons within the meaning of the section and that the club was not established for the sole purpose of promoting sport but also or mainly for the purpose of avoiding tax.

Held The entire contract of the club was vested by its constitution in the defendants and club 349 was thus a proprietary club in the ownership of the defendants. Accordingly, the defendants must constitute the body of persons mentioned in s. 349 to avail of its provisions. The only expressions which could apply to the club were fellowship of persons or society of persons and in the context in which the expressions are used two persons cannot constitute a body of persons within the meaning of s. 349.

Cases referred to in judgment
Director of Public Prosecutions v Luft & Anor [1976] 3 WLR 32
Irish Permanent Building Society v Registrar of Building Societies, Irish Life Building Society and Others [1981] ILRM 242

Reported at [1983] ILRM 34   (Appeal to the Supreme Court dismissed.)

ROAD TRAFFIC ACT

Director of Public Prosecutions (Long) v McDonald and Others *and* O'Mahony and Others v Biggs and Others: Supreme Court 1979 Nos. 19 & 20 (Walsh J, Henchy and Griffin JJ) 22 July 1982 (Nem. Diss.)

Road Traffic - Street traders - Conviction for breach of byelaws made for the control of traffic - Whether vehicle being used in connection with the sale of goods in a lawful market - Presumption of immemorial usage from which a lost grant presumed - Constitution of Ireland 1937, Art. 40.3 - Road Traffic Act, 1961, (No. 24), ss. 89(1), 89(7), 90(1), 92.

Facts S. 89 of the Road Traffic Act 1961 empowers the making of bye-laws for the regulation and control of traffic and pedestrians, and s. 90 empowers the making of bye-laws for the control and regulation of the parking of vehicles on public roads. S. 92 of the Act provides for the making of bye-laws to provide free passage of vehicular traffic through public roads on the occasion of fairs or markets. The defendant street traders in the instant two sets of cases sold their wares at fairs and markets using their motor vehicles as mobile shops and were prosecuted and convicted in the District Court for breaches of bye-laws made under ss. 89 and 90. They appealed unsuccessfully by way of case stated to the High Court and now appealed to the Supreme Court contending (1) the bye-laws were bad for being unreasonable (2) they were bad for lack of good faith in their making and (3) that bye-laws under ss. 89 and 90 were not applicable to the circumstances of these cases. The defendants in the first set of cases had each parked a motor van in connection with the sale of goods at Barrack Street, Carlow where a market carried on theretofore at Tullow St. from 1950 and which had moved to Barrack St. at the request of the Garda Siochana had been carried on since 1956 though under no statute or express grant. The defendants in the second set of cases had contravened bye-laws made under ss. 89 and 90 by parking their vans in Grattan Square, Dungarvan for over one hour during a market. Uncontradicted evidence showed that a market had been held during living memory in the square on the third Wednesday of each month.

Held (Henchy J, Griffin, Walsh JJ concurring) Submissions (1) and (2) were not supported by the evidence. On the facts when a market had been held for such a long period as the market at Barrack St. there was a presumption of immemorial usage from which a lost grant might be presumed and the holding of a regular market uninterruptedly there since 1956 and indeed elsewhere since 1950 raised the presumption that it was a lawful market. The evidence established that there had been a lawful market at Grattan Square on the occasion of each of the offences giving rise to the second set of cases. In each set of cases, bye-laws made under s. 92 would be required to make the conduct complained of unlawful. Since the only bye-laws relied on by the prosecution in each set of cases were made under ss. 89 and 90 which were accordingly not applicable the appeals in each of the two cases stated would be allowed.

No cases referred to in judgment.

Reported at [1983] ILRM 223

SALE OF GOODS

In the Matter of The Companies Act, 1963 *and* **In the Matter of Galway Concrete Ltd (In Liquidation):** High Court 1981 No. 3311P (Keane J) 10 December 1982.

Sale of Goods - Retention of title clause - Suppliers entering into a leasing contract of plant machinery with bank - Purchasing company going into liquidation - Application by liquidator for directions as to the rights of the three parties - Whether plant by reasons of being affixed to the land became part of the land - Whether plant merely tenant's fixtures - No express provision in agreement of sale empowering suppliers to repossess in the event of default - Whether such term to be implied and whether purchasing company to bear costs of removal of plant - Whether charge created by retention of title clause - Companies Act 1963 (33), s. 99

Facts The company in liquidation ordered in March 1979 a batching plant consisting of *inter alia* two cement silos and two cement screw conveyors and installed it in its premises in Galway in September 1979. The terms of the purchase provided *inter alia* for payment of the purchase sum of £105,000.00 by five equal annual payments of £21,000.00. It was further provided that the goods were to remain the property of the suppliers until the purchase price had been paid in full. Payment of the second annual sum was stopped by the company and the suppliers demanded repossession of the plant which the company withheld. The company went in liquidation in April 1979. In September 1979 a finance house agreed to appoint the suppliers their agent to purchase the equipment and reimburse the suppliers in respect of the purchase by payment of £103,939.00 and entered a leasing contract under which the suppliers agreed to take the plant on lease for an initial period of 48 months. The liquidator applied to the court for directions as to the rights of the company the suppliers and the finance house. Evidence was adduced to show that the plant had been substantially incorporated in the company's premises and the liquidator contended that (i) the plant had become part thereof under the maxim *quid quid plantatur solo solo cedit* and that accordingly the retention of title clause in the agreement was of no effect, (ii) the arrangement between the suppliers and the finance house divested the suppliers of any entitlement to the chattels and (iii) if the property in the plant passed to the owner of the land that the finance house could have no title to it. The suppliers contended that the component parts of the plant had been affixed to the land to carry on the companys trade and were therefore tenants fixtures and removable at any time and that the right to remove them remained vested in the suppliers under the original agreement with the company. The finance house contended that this right had become vested in them under the arrangements with the suppliers.

Held The plant had become so affixed to the land as to become part of it but since on the facts this was for the purposes of the companys trade it was in the nature of a tenants fixture which could be removed by the tenant. Although the agreement between the company and the suppliers did not contain any clause empowering the suppliers to repossess the goods in the event of a default in payment by the company there was no doubt that it was intended that the supplier should have that right. Since the supplier's right to require the company to sever the chattels which had become tenant's fixtures, or to avail themselves of the right to enter and sever them did not depend on the existence of a clause expressly conferring a right to repossession, and since the company had clearly repudiated the agreement the suppliers had become entitled to remove the plant. However since it was intended that the property in the plant should vest in the finance house when the finance house reimbursed the suppliers in respect of the purchase price, the finance house and not the suppliers were now the owners of the plant and the right to enter and remove the plant was now vested in the finance house. Since the removal of the plant was a necessary consequence of the companys breach of the agreement with the suppliers they were liable to pay damages in respect of the breach and the finance house were accordingly entitled to recover the costs of removing the plant as damages for breach of contract.

Cases referred to in judgment
Becker v Riebold 30 TLR 142
Borden (UK) Ltd v Scottish Timber Products Ltd and Anor [1979] 3 All ER 961
Crossley Bros. v Lee [1980] I KB 86
In Re Bond Worth Ltd [1980] Ch 228
Frigoscandia (Contracting) Ltd v Continental Irish Meat and Crowley [1982] ILRM 396

Authorities cited in legal argument
Appleby and Anor v Myers LR 2CP 651
Goode on Hire Purchase Law and Practice at 736
Hudson's Building and Engineering Contracts 10th Edition, 655

Reported at [1983] ILRM 402

SALE OF LAND

Daniel Crean v David Drinan: High Court 1979 No. 3680P (Barrington J) 22 May 1982

Sale of Land - Contract subject to vendor remedying any possible defects in title before closing date - Vendor unable to comply - Purchaser deciding not to proceed - Claim for return of deposit - Interpretation of agreement - whether time of the essence.

Facts The plaintiff purchaser contracted with the defendant vendor for the sale of a public house as a going concern. The closing date was to be 4 May 1979 and the plaintiff paid a deposit of £9,000. Special condition no. 2 provided that the contract was to be subject to the defendant obtaining an assignment of any outstanding interest in the property that might have been vested in certain third parties in a form acceptable to the plaintiff's solicitors on or before the closing date. It was further provided that in the event of the deed not being executed the purchaser should be refunded his deposit but without interest, costs or compensation of any kind. An engrossed assignment was sent to the defendant's solicitor prior to the closing date, but on 15 May the plaintiff's solicitor was informed that the assignment had not yet been completed and that one of the third parties was abroad on holidays. The plaintiff thereupon decided not to proceed with the sale and sought the return of his deposit which the defendant witheld.

Held The production by the vendor of the assignment referred to, duly executed by the third parties on or before 4 May, was a condition precedent to the operation of the contract as a contract for sale. On the failure of the vendor to produce this deed the purchaser was discharged from his obligation and was entitled to the refund of his deposit without interest, costs or compensation. Since the plaintiff, on being informed of his rights, immediately refused to go ahead with the sale, he could not be held to have waived his rights under condition 2 or to have revived the contract.

Cases referred to in judgment
Aberfoyle Plantations Ltd v Cheng [1960] AC 115; [1959] 3 WLR 1011;
Re Sandwell Park Colliery Co [1929] 1 Ch 277; [1928] All ER 651
Maloney v Elf Investments Ltd High Court 1979 No. 295sp (McWilliam J) 7 December 1979
Property and Bloodstock Ltd v Emerton [1967] 2 All ER 839

Cases referred to in legal argument
Buckland and Others v Farmer and Moody [1979] 1 WLR 380; [1978] 3 All ER 929 CA
O'Brien v Seaview Enterprises Ltd High Court (Circuit Appeal) (Finlay P) 31 May 1976.

Reported at [1983] ILRM 82

Roberts v O'Neill and Anor: Supreme Court 1981 No. 221 (O'Higgins CJ Hederman and McCarthy JJ) 8 December 1982 Nem. Diss.

Sale of Land - Specific Performance - Negotiations with two potential purchasers for sale of licensed premises - Formal contract drawn up with second potential purchaser - First potential purchaser alleging existence of prior enforceable agreement - Institution of proceedings for specific performance - Claim dismissed - Second potential purchaser now seeking to complete sale - Whether appropriate to order specific performance.

Facts In January 1978 the defendants made a contract with the plaintiff to sell him their public house. Before completion of this contract one Carthy commenced an action, which was later dismissed, against the defendants claiming specific performance of another alleged contract for the sale of the same public house to him. In March 1978 the plaintiff commenced an action for specific performance. In May 1981 the first defendant filed an amended defence and counterclaim in which it was pleaded for the first time that the public house had increased greatly in value, as had public houses generally, since the contract of sale and that it would be unjust if the defendants were obliged to sell at the contract price. The High Court granted an order for specific performance against both defendants and the first defendant appealed, arguing that damages should be awarded in lieu of specific performance. He further argued that he would be unable to buy another public house to continue as a publican and that his son would be unable to have a career as a publican and that the discretion to refuse specific performance should be exercised on the basis of hardship existing at the date of trial and not at the date of the contract.

Held The appeal would be dismissed. An examination of the evidence threw doubt on the reality of the alleged claim of hardship. The rule is that only harsdhip existing at the time of the contract may ground a refusal of specific performance. There may be rare cases of hardship arising after the contract where the court should interfere with the contract and, in order to do justice should over-ride strictly legal principles and the well-recognised procedures of the courts of equity but this was not one of them and such cases would not ordinarily include cases of hardship arising from inflation alone.

Cases referred to in judgment
Lavan v Walsh [1964] IR 87
Nial Fennelly SC and John Gallagher **for the first defendant/appellant.**
Raymond O'Neill SC, T. C. Smyth SC and William Hamill **for the plaintiff/respondent.**

Reported at [1983] ILRM 206

Valentine Keating, Arthur Molloy and George Roe v Bank of Ireland and Reginald A. C. Brentland and Heather B. King: High Court 1981 No. 8823P (Barrington J) 30 July 1982.

Vendor and Purchaser - Contract for sale of land - General Conditions of Sale - Claim by purchaser for compensation for misdescription - Whether purchasers obliged to complete sale pending resolution of such claim, by arbitration - Equity.

Facts The defendants had contracted to sell certain lands to the plaintiffs for £306,000. The contract incorporated the 1978 edition of the General Conditions of Sale of the Incorporated Law Society. The plaintiffs brought this action claiming damages for fraud and misrepresentation, and also specific performance with a £100,000 abatement of the purchase price to compensate for error, omission or mis-statement. The defendants counterclaimed for specific performance of the contract in accordance with its terms. The parties went to arbitration on the question of whether condition 21 of the General Conditions applied and on the amount of compensation, if any, to which the plaintiffs were entitled. The High Court ordered the trial of 3 issues in the form of 3 questions. Question (1) was whether, if the plaintiffs were successful in the claim for compensation under Condition 21, they were entitled to a sum to be awarded by way of compensation by way of an abatement of the purchase price; Question (2) was whether the vendors were entitled to insist upon completion before determination of the dispute relating to compensation. Question (3) was whether, if the answer to (2) was in the negative, the vendors were entitled to insist upon completion prior to the determination of the said dispute with the vendors agreeing to hold on joint deposit pending the outcome of the dispute the amount claimed by way of compensation by the plaintiffs. The plaintiff submitted that condition 21 must be read in the light of the traditional understanding of the law concerning compensation and abatement for misdescription. They submitted that 'abatement' has traditionally meant a reduction in the purchase price ascertained prior to completion, and compensation was merely the amount of the abatement. The defendants submitted that the purchasers had a duty to complete immediately and to leave the amount in dispute on joint deposit to await the outcome of the arbitration.

Held If the plaintiffs were entitled to compensation, they were entitled to it out of the purchase money, and they could not be forced to close until the amount of compensation, if any, and therefore until the price payable had been ascertained. The 3 questions would be answered as follows (1) Yes. (2) No. (3) No.

Cases referred to in judgment
Connor v Potts [1897] 1 IR 534
Cordingly v Cheeseborough (1862) LJ Vol. 31 Ch Ns 617
Denton v Stewart (1786) 1 Coxes Equity Cases 258
Grant v Dawhins & Ors [1973] 3 All ER 897
Northern Bank Ltd v Duffy [1981] ILRM 308

Reported at [1983] ILRM 295

Margaret Weir v Sandra Somers: Supreme Court 1982 No. 256 (O'Higgins CJ, Finlay P, McCarthy J) 18 March 1983 *(nem. diss.)*

Sale of Land - Conveyance of family home without consent of wife - Purchaser taking up residence - Supreme Court declaring conveyance void - Application by wife for possession - Whether Supreme Court order vested leasehold interest in wife - Family Home Protection Act, 1976 (No. 27) s. 3(1), 4(1), 5.

Facts The plaintiff's husband was legal owner of premises known as No. 111, Maryfield Crescent, Artane, Dublin. The plaintiff had resided in the premises with her husband and their children, but she left to live elsewhere in 1973. In November 1974 the plaintiff and her husband entered into a separation agreement. The agreement made no provision for or any reference to the ownership of the family home. In August 1976 the husband entered into a written agreement with the defendant assigning his leasehold interest in the premises. Prior to completion of the sale and in the temporary absence of the husband, the defendant's solicitor prepared a statutory declaration stating that the plaintiff had no interest in the premises by virtue of the separation agreement of 1974. The statutory declaration was duly executed by the husband on his return, and the sale was closed some days later. The defendant then agreed to resell the premises in April 1977 to a third party who discovered that there had been no consent in writing by the plaintiff to the conveyance of 1976 from the plaintiff's husband. The defendant failed to obtain the plaintiff's consent retrospectively and instituted proceedings entitled Somers v W. [1979] IR 94 in the High Court seeking a declaration dispensing with the consent of the plaintiff pursuant to

s. 4 of the Family Home Protection Act, 1976. The Supreme Court in reversing the order of the High Court held that the purported conveyance in 1976 by the husband to the defendant was void. The plaintiff then sued her husband for a declaration of her interest in the premises, and subsequently commenced Circuit Court proceedings claiming an injunction to eject Mrs Somers and any other occupiers of the premises from residing in occupation of them. Meanwhile in the further action brought by Mrs Weir against her husband, D'Arcy J by order of 24 June 1981 declared:

> (a) That the premises 111, Maryfield Crescent, Artane in the County of Dublin is a family home as between the plaintiff and the defendant, and,
> (b) That the plaintiff is entitled to a half share in the leasehold interest in the said premises.

The Circuit Court proceedings subsequently came before Judge Noel Ryan on 12 February 1982, who then posed certain questions by way of case stated to the Supreme Court. All of the questions related to the previous action held between the respective parties. The questions posed in the case stated were *inter alia* as follows:
  (i) Did the said order of the Supreme Court vest the leasehold interest in the family home in the plaintiff?
  (ii) Did the order of the said D'Arcy J vest the leasehold interest in the family home in the plaintiff?
  (iii) Does the said order of the Supreme Court referred to entitle the plaintiff to the relief sought in these proceedings?
  (iv) Does the estate or interest referred to in the order of D'Arcy J entitle the plaintiff to the relief sought in these proceedings?

Held by McCarthy J, (O'Higgins CJ and Finlay P concurring):
  1. While the order of the Supreme Court does not vest the leasehold interest in the plaintiff it can be necessarily inferred from the said order that the premises are the 'family home' within the meaning of the Act of 1976.
  2. The order of D'Arcy J entitled the plaintiff to a half share in the leasehold of the premises, the plaintiff was thereby entitled to have the legal estate in such a half share conveyed to her and should be treated as the person having such legal estate. Payment by the defendant to Terence Weir as a purported purchase price did not create an estate or interest in the premises in the defendant, nor had she then any defence in these proceedings.
  3. The Circuit Court judge would have no option but to grant the injunction sought so as to ensure that the plaintiff and her family obtained immediate possession of the premises.

Case referred to in judgment
Somers v W [1979] IR 94

Reported at [1983] ILRM 343

Finbarr J. Crowley v John Flynn: High Court 1982 No. 525 SP (Barron J) 13 May 1983.

Vendor and Purchaser - Leasehold interest in property - Interest bequeathed to testatrix's executor upon trust for sale - Delay - Upon executor's death letters of administration de bonis non obtained by testatrix's two daughters - Contract for the sale of the interest - Purchaser refusing to accept title from administratices de bonis non - whether vendor, selling as personal representative, must satisfy the purchaser that he has power to sell as such - Whether assent to the establishment of a trust for sale should be inferred - Succession Act 1965 (No. 27), s. 51(1).

Facts The testatrix Maude Robb died on 15 May 1946 having by her last will dated 4 March 1943 bequeathed her leasehold interest in certain property to her executor and trustee George Robb on trust for sale and to hold proceeds of sale as to two-sixteenths for himself and the balance to be divided equally between her two daughters. A grant of probate was obtained on 11 July 1946. George Robb died on 24 August 1978 and letters of administration *de bonis non* were obtained by the deceased's two daughters on 20 March 1981. Following a contract for sale of the leasehold interest dated 7 August 1979 the purchaser refused to accept title from the administratices de bonis non. It was submitted on behalf of the purchaser that: (i) no power of sale had been shown to subsist because no reason had been given for the exercise of such power by personal representatives after the lapse of 33 years, and, (ii) that the delay had been such that an assent to the establishment of the will trust should be inferred. The vendor submitted that, (i) an executor is always entitled to sell for the purposes of distribution of the assets among the beneficiaries, and (ii) that a purchaser would in any event be protected by the provisions of s. 51 of The Succession Act 1965.

Held by Barron J
1. As more than twenty years had elapsed since the death of the testator, the purchaser was put on notice to enquire the reason for sale. There was nothing in s. 51 of the Succession Act 1965, which suggests that a purchaser is never to be put upon enquiry.
2. As there was doubt on the facts as to the proper inference to be drawn from the delay it was not a title which the court would compel a purchaser to accept.
3. A good title to the hereditments had not been shown in accordance with the particulars and conditions of sale.

Cases referred to in judgment
George Attenborough & Son v Solomon [1913] AC 76
Molyneux v White 15 LRI 383
Norwood v Blake's Contract 1917 IR 472
Somers v Weir [1979] IR 94
Wise v Whitburn [1924] 1 Ch 460

Reported at [1983] ILRM 513

STATUTE OF LIMITATIONS

James B. Bellew v Bryan B. Baron Bellew and Bryan E. Bellew: Supreme Court 1981 No 181 (O'Higgins CJ, Griffin and Hederman JJ) 21 April 1982.

Statute of Limitations - Occupation of lands with approval and consent of owner - Occupation continuing beyond what was originally contemplated to the exclusion of the owner - Nature of occupation - Whether as a result of a licence or a tenancy at will - Adverse possession - Whether owner's title extinguished - Statute of Limitations 1957 (No. 6) ss 13(2); 17(1), 18, 24, 51(1).

Facts Fifth Baron Bellew (brother of first defendant) owned Barmeath Castle and grounds in fee simple. First defendant, on the urging of brother went to live at Barmeath and made it his home in 1939. He was given a yearly tenancy of the house; he was joined there in 1949 by the plaintiff (his son) with his wife and family (including the second defendant). In 1953, fifth Baron Bellew conveyed the entire property to the plaintiff subject to the existing tenancy in the house in favour of the first defendant. In 1960, the plaintiff executed a deed of settlement, settling the house and the lands on himself for life with remainder to the second defendant in tail with remainder over. This settlement was also subject to the existing tenancy. In June 1961, the plaintiff left Barmeath never to return because of an affair with another woman and left his wife and family behind him without providing for their welfare. After negotiations over some months, it was proposed between solicitors for the plaintiff and the first defendant that a lease of the lands be executed in favour of the first defendant and subject thereto for a conveyance of the plaintiff's life interest to the second defendant, the first defendant agreeing to support the plaintiff's wife, and family. These negotiations broke down in July 1963, and all communication between the plaintiff and those at Barmeath ceased. The plaintiff then commenced divorce proceedings in London. In December 1977, the first defendant became the sixth Baron Bellew on the death of his brother and he and the plaintiff's wife made a lease of the lands to the second defendant for 21 years from 18 December 1977, together with a supplementary lease for the same term to the plaintiff's second son. When the leases came to the attention of the plaintiff, he commenced proceedings claiming that he had a life interest in the property and that the defendants had no interest.

Held (by O'Higgins CJ) that the second defendant's occupation of the property created a tenancy at will, which determined (under s. 17(1)(a) of the 1957 Act) one year after its commencement. Second defendant was in adverse possession after that, and as that period exceeded 12 years, the plaintiff's title was extinguished (under s. 24 of the Act).
Griffin J and Hederman J concurring.

Cases referred to in judgment
Cobb v Lane [1952] 1 All ER 1199

Doe v Chamberlain (1839) 5 M&W 14
Fachini v Bryson [1951] 1 TLR 1386 CA
Gatien Motor Co v Continental Oil [1979] IR 406
Heslop v Burns [1974] 1 WLR 1241; [1974] 3 All ER 406 CA
Hughes v Griffin [1969] 1 WLR 23
Lynes v Snaith [1899] 1 QB 486
Murphy v Murphy [1980] IR 183
Perry v Woodfarm Homes Ltd., [1975] IR 104
Shell-Mex v Manchester Garages Ltd [1971] 1 WLR 612

Reported at [1983] ILRM 128

Brian Morgan v Park Developments Ltd: High Court 1980 No. 4381P (Carroll J) 2 February 1983

Statute of limitations - Defective premises - House built on unsuitable foundations developing structural fault - Date when cause of action accrued - Whether date of damage or date of discoverability of damage - Whether date of accrual further extended on the grounds of equitable estoppel or fraudulent concealment - Statute of Limitations 1957 (No. 6), ss. 11(1), 11(2)(a), 71(1)

Facts The plaintiff purchased a house from the defendants, building contractors in 1962. Shortly after moving into occupation the plaintiff notified the defendants of defects which had occurred in the premises. The defendants repaired the defects including a large crack in the corner of the house which reappeared and required further repairs by the defendants in 1965. About this time the plaintiff was informed by the defendant's agent, the site foreman, that the crack was merely a settlement crack and that it would take some years to settle. The plaintiff did nothing further until in 1975 when he had an extension built to the house and his contractor unsuccessfully attempted to repair the wall as the crack subsequently reappeared.

In 1979 the plaintiff consulted an architect who told him that the problem was with the foundations of the house which had resulted in a major structural fault. Proceedings were issued in 1980. The defendants claimed that the plaintiff's case was statute barred and that the proper date of accrual of a right of action was when the damage had occurred and when the breach of contract was committed. For the plaintiff, it was submitted that the date of accrual was when the damage was discoverable and that this had been postponed by reason of the representation made by the defendant's agent who had lulled the plaintiff into a false sense of security, sufficient to preclude the defendant's from pleading the statute.

Held (1) The date of accrual in the action for negligence in the building of a house is the date the defect either was discovered or should have reasonably been discovered.

(2) The date of accrual of the right of action under the plaintiff's contract with the defendant, was the date in 1965 when the defendants had finished the remedial works.
(3) Neither date of accrual would be sufficient to bring the plaintiff's claim within the six year period allowed by the statute of limitations 1957.
(4) The assurances given by the defendants agent was merely a statement of opinion and not sufficient to enable the plaintiff to prove fraudulent concealment. Within the meaning of s. 71(1)(b) of the statute of limitations the defendants were not stopped from seeking to non-suit the plaintiff. The plaintiff had acted unreasonably an ' with undue delay in failing to take the proper remedial action.

Cases referred to in judgment.
Anns v Merton London Borough Council [1977] 2 WLR 1024
Buckley v Lynch [1978] IR 6
Colgan v Connolly Construction Co Ltd High Court 1979 No. 2008P (McMahon J) 29 February 1980
Cartledge v E. Jopling & Sons Ltd [1963] AC 758
Doran v Thomas Thompson & Sons Ltd [1978] IR 223
Howell v Young (1826) 5 B and C 259
King v Victor Parsons & Co [1973] 1 WLR 29
Kitchen v Royal Air Force Assoc. [1958] 1 WLR 563
Pirelli General Cable Works Ltd v Oscar Faber & Partners [1983] 2 WLR 6
Siney v Dublin Corporation [1980] IR 400
Sparham-Souter v Town and Country Developments (Essex) Ltd and Anor [1976] 2 WLR 493

Reported at [1983] ILRM 156   [This case is under appeal]

Alfie Smith v Ireland, the Attorney General and the Pigs and Bacon Commission: High Court 1982 No. 1113P (Finlay P) 11 February 1983.

Statute of Limitations - Pigs and Bacon Commission - Claim in respect of deductions made by Commission - Whether claim statute barred - Limitation period having expired - Whether acknowledgement - Whether defendants estopped from pleading the statute - Whether European Community Law prohibits defendants from pleading the statute - Statute of Limitations 1957, (No. 6) ss 3(1), 56(1) - European Communities Act, 1972, (No. 27) s. 2.

Facts In 1972 the plaintiff sold pigs to certain licensed pig factories. When the plaintiff later submitted a claim for payment to the Department of Agriculture and Fisheries he was notified by return that no payment could be made until the plaintiff could prove the origin of the pigs to the satisfiaction of the Minister. No further correspondence was entered into until 30 December 1975 when the plaintiff again requested payment. The Minister replied on 5 January 1976 acknowledging the receipt of the letter, and indicating that the matter would receive consideration in due course. In the intervening period another pig producer had commenced an action against the Pigs and Bacon Commission and the Department of Agriculture and Fisheries claiming a declaration that certain Statutory Instruments fixing minimum prices for pigs in 1972 were invalid. That action was heard in the High Court in 1978, and not ultimately disposed of until 1980. In 1982 the plaintiff issued a summary summons against the defendants claiming £16,320. The action was remitted for plenary hearing, and the sole issue before the court was whether the plaintiff's claim was statute barred. In arguing against the defence based on the Statute of Limitations, 1957 the plaintiff claimed:

1. That the letter written on behalf of the Minister on 5 January 1976 had constituted an acknowledgement of the debt by the defendants, and that this was sufficient to defeat the statute.
2. Alternatively, that the plaintiff had refrained from issuing proceedings in the belief that the defendants in correspondence would eventually accept liability for the plaintiff's claim, and that the defendants were therefore estopped from pleading the statute.
3. That the defendants, in correspondence with the plaintiff had entitled the plaintiff to a legitimate expectation that his claim would be satisfactorily discharged by the defendants in due course. This claim, it was submitted, entitled him to rely on certain principles of European Community law, and in particular the prohibition therein contained against the defeating of legitimate expectation and against discrimination or inequality in the treatment of agricultural producers.

Held by Finlay P in dismissing the plaintiff's claim:
1. It was statute barred, at the latest, after December 1978 by virtue of the provisions of s. 11 of the Statute of Limitations, 1957.
2. The defendant's correspondence with the plaintiff did not constitute an acknowledgement of a debt owing to the plaintiff; there could be no such acknowledgement in the absence of a liquidated or quantified figure capable of ascertaining the amount of the debt without further agreement of the parties.
3. The defendants were not estopped from relying on pleading the Statute of Limitations. The correspondence did not constitute an encouragement of the plaintiff to defer his action against the defendants in the belief that they would ultimately accept responsibility for the claim.
4. As regards the plaintiff's third submission, the plaintiff had failed to prove any legitimate expectation or inequality or discrimination.

Cases referred to in judgment
Crabb v Arun District Council [1975] 3 All ER 865
Good v Parry [1963] 2 All ER 59
McCrumlish v The Minister for Agriculture High Court 1972 No. 349P (Gannon J) 28 May 1975
Willmott v Barber (1880) Ch. D. 96

Reported at [1983] ILRM 300

SUCCESSION

MH and N McG v NM and CM: High Court 1978 No. 7524P (Barron J) 2 March 1983

Succession - Will - Construction - Testator and wife owning shares in the company used to run their business - Wife predeceasing testator - Her estate left unadministered - Testator leaving "all my shares and interests in the business" to two of his children - Residue of the estate left to his remaining four children - Whether testator's proportion of the shares in the company held by his wife, which would have passed to him on completion of the administration of her estate, passed under the specific bequest to his two children or under the residuary bequest to his remaining children -

Succession - Will - Whether testator failed to make proper provision for his children - Succession Act 1965 (No. 27), s. 117 -

Facts The testator died in 1977, having made his will in 1976. His wife had died intestate in 1973. At his death, he owned 300 of the 1,000 issued shares in a company which ran a public house. His wife had held 300 of these shares and his sons CM and RM each owned 200 shares. His wife's estate was left unadministered. By his will the testator left his house, its contents and all 'my shares and interests in the business of licensed vintners carried on therein under the name of CM and Sons Ltd' to his two sons NM and CM and the residue to his remaining 4 children. The residue was worthless therefore NM and CM effectively got the entire estate.

A question of construction arose as to whether the testator's proportion of the shares held by his deceased wife, which would have passed to him on completion of the administration of her estate, passed under the specific bequest to NM and CM and under the residuary bequest to the remaining 4 children.

MH and N McG, 2 daughters, the plaintiffs in these proceedings, claimed under s. 117 of the Succession Act, 1965 that the testator, their father, had failed to make proper provision for them in his will, which had effectively left them nothing and everything to NM and CM. The two remaining children DK and RM, made no claim under s. 117. N. McG was born in 1945 and was married in 1970. Her husband had a job. MH was born in 1948 and married in 1968. Her husband's business had had some difficulty but she was in reasonably good financial circumstances. N McG was in less good financial circumstances but expressed herself to be contented with her position. NM was born in 1933 and CM in 1944. NM certainly and CM to some degree, had given up independent employment to go into the family business in the public house. To that extent their careers were moulded by their expectations from their parents. The main basis of the plaintiff's claim was that they had been brought up very frugally, that they had looked after their mother in her two illnesses and that NM and CM would have capital behind them whereas they would not.

Held On the question of construction of the will, the 200 shares to which the testator would have become entitled upon the completion of the administration of his wife's estate, did not became his shares. He did, however, acquire a specific interest in them which passed to his executor. They would not have passed under a bequest of 'my shares', however they did pass under the bequest of 'all my interest in the business' in relation to the claim under s. 117 of the Succession Act, the testator had not failed to make proper provision for the plaintiffs. Proper provision for NM and CM required such provision as would permit the continuation of their livelihoods from the business.

Cases referred to in judgment
Cooper v Cooper LR 7 HL 53
H v H 1981 No. 1042 Sp (Gannon J) 2 March 1983
Re Leigh's Will Trusts, Handyside and Anor v Durbridge and Others [1969] 3 All ER 432; [1970] Ch 277
Tevlin v Gilsenen [1902] 1 IR 514
Vanneck v Benham [1917] 1 Ch 60
Villiers v Holmes [1917] 1 IR 165

'Reported at [1983] ILRM 519

TORT

Adidas Sportschuhfabriken Adi Dassler KA v Charles O'Neill & Co Ltd: Supreme Court 1980 No. 174 (O'Higgins CJ, Henchy and Hederman JJ) 2 July 1982.

Tort - Passing off - Foreign company with international trading reputation marketing sportswear with distinctive design - Irish company using similar design - Neither design registered as a trademark - Whether plaintiffs could claim any exclusive property or reputation in respect of the design - Whether defendants passing off their goods as those of the plaintiffs - Whether mere copying of a design or taking advantage of a demand created by another's advertising sufficient to support an action for passing off.

Facts Adidas (the plaintiff) commenced operations in 1947 as manufacturer and distributor of sports footwear which was marked with a distinctive design and fashion of three diagonal coloured stripes on each boot. In 1967 Adidas began to manufacture sportswear such as tracksuits which had a distinctive three stripe design down the sides of the arms and legs of the tracksuits and jerseys manufactured by that company. In 1976, the plaintiff began manufacturing their products in Ireland which brought them into competition with the defendants (O'Neill & Co). The defendants were long established in the Irish sports market, manufacturing its own sports apparel. In 1965 O'Neill began putting stripes on its products. The number of stripes varied on what was ordered from 1 to 3 but within a few years it concentrated on a three stripe design. Evidence was given at the trial that the three stripe design has been used by manufacturers of sports wear in many other countries, but that Adidas were the only manufacturers who exclusively used the particular arrangement of light coloured stripes of equal width set against a differently coloured background. Adidas claimed that O'Neill by the use of the three striped design in the manner stated was passing off the products as the products of Adidas. The defendant claimed that the Adidas three striped design was not part of the goodwill of Adidas. To establish such a claim for passing off the plaintiff would have to prove that he had an exclusive association with a particular design on its products in Ireland.

In the High Court it was held by MacWilliam J that the plaintiff had failed to establish essential reputation in Ireland in relation to the three stripe design and that no confusion had been caused by the defendant's use of the three stripe design.

Held By O'Higgins CJ, Hederman J concurring dismissing the appeal.
1. The use of the stripes of varying colours and numbers on sports garments was a fashion in the trade and that the defendants in resorting to fashionable demands had not attempted to deceive or pass off and had in fact not done so.
2. **Held** by Henchy J dissenting
1. In allowing the appeal and granting the plaintiffs an injunction restraining the defendant from selling or offering for sale sports garments bearing the three stripe arrangement to be found on such garments when manufactured by or for Adidas.
3. The evidence at the trial of the action was sufficient to sustain the plaintiffs claim that the three stripe design had become part of the goodwill of Adidas.
4. The plaintiffs had acquired a recognised and protectible property right which was sufficient to entitle them to a common law trade mark (apart from registration of a trade mark) protectible by a passing off action.

Cases referred to in judgment
Alain Bernadin v Pavilion Properties Ltd (1976) RPC 581
Cadbury-Schweppes v Pub Squash Co [1981] WLR 193; [1981] 1 All ER 213
C & A Modes v C & A Waterford Ltd and Others [1976] IR 198
Lever Brothers v Bedingfield (1898) 15 RPC 453
Oertli AG v Bowman (London) Ltd (1957) RPC 388
Schweppes Ltd v Gibbons (1905) 22 RPC 601
Revenue Commissioners v Muller & Co's Margarine Ltd [1901] AC 217

Reported at [1983] ILRM 112

Coras Iompair Eireann v Michael Carroll and Wexford County Council:
High Court 1976 No. 4925P (Gannon J) 14 June 1982

Tort - negligence - nuisance - road accident - destruction of overhead bridge - derailment of train - apportionment of blame as between defendants - Clearance between road surface and underside of the bridge less than the prescribed statutory dimension - Whether breach of plaintiff's statutory duty - Diminution in clearance due to road works carried out by second defendant - Railway Clauses Consolidation Act 1845, (Ch. 20) ss. 46, 49, 52-57, Local Government Act (No. 5) 1925, Part III

Facts A mechanical digger owned and driven by the first defendant collided with a railway bridge the property of the plaintiff. The plaintiff claimed against the first defendant for negligence, and against the second defendant for negligence and nuisance in relation to the construction and maintenance of the road, and for the failure to give a suitable warning to road traffic of the nature of the road and bridge clearance. The defendants claimed that ss. 46 and 49 of the Railway Clauses Consolidation Act, 1845 imposed on the plaintiffs a statutory duty to maintain a 15 ft. clearance between the under side of the bridge and the road. The case was heard by a judge sitting without a jury to determine preliminary issues or questions of law and fact relating to the apportionment of liability. It was established during the trial that over a course of time the second defendant raised the surface of the road level beneath the bridge thereby reducing the clearance to less than 15 ft without having any particular regard to the nature of the traffic likely to use the road.

Held by Gannon J
(i) There was no negligence or breach of any statutory duty on the part of the plaintiff.
(ii) Negligence was apportioned between the defendants on the basis of 90% to the first defendant and 10% to the second defendant.
(iii) At the time of the accident the first defendant was exclusively in control of the circumstances under which the damage complained of could have been avoided.
(iv) There was no statutory obligation on the second defendant to maintain the 15 ft. clearance under the bridge but by reducing the clearance the second defendant incurred the risk of damage to the plaintiff's bridge. The risk should have been foreseen in the course of the normal discharge of their functions as road authority conversant with the development of traffic.
(v) The second defendant's failure to provide advance warning after having reduced the clearance was a breach of duty which contributed in some measure to creating the circumstances of risk of damage.

Cases referred to in judgment and legal argument
Attorney General v Furness Railway 47 LJ Ch. 776
Attorney General (Pickfords Ltd) v Great Northern Railway [1916] 2 AC 356
Attorney General for Ireland v Lagan Canal Co [1924] AC 877
Fosberry v Wexford and Limerick Railway Co. 13 ICLR 494
Kearney v London and Brighton Railway IR 6QB 759
Lewis v Burnett [1945] 2 All ER 555
London and North Western Railway Co. v Skelton (1864) 5 B &S 559
Monmouthshire County Council v British Transport Commission [1957] 1 All ER 662; 3 All ER 384 CA.
McKenna v Lewis & Laois County Council [1945] IR 66
North Staffordshire Railway Co v Dale 8E and B 836
Swain v Southern Railway Co. [1939] 2 All ER 794
Wexford and Limerick Railway Co v Kearney 12 ICLR 224
Reported at [1983] ILRM 173

Aidan O'Dowd v The North Western Health Board: Supreme Court 1981 No. 4 (O'Higgins CJ, Henchy and Griffin JJ) 16 July 1982.

Tort - Detention of person as being of unsound mind - Subsequent discharge - Person then seeking to institute proceedings arising out of his detention - Requirement that person show substantial grounds for contending that the Board, through its officers, acted in bad faith or without reasonable care - Whether claim made out - Meaning of 'substantial' - Mental Treatment Act, 1945 (No. 19), s. 260.

Facts S. 26, of the Mental Treatment Act, 1945 provides that no civil proceedings shall be instituted in respect of an act purporting to have been done in pursuance of that act save by leave of the High Court and that such leave shall not be granted unless the High Court is satisfied that there are substantial grounds for contending that the person against whom the proceedings are to be brought acted in bad faith or without reasonable care. (The onus of proof necessary to sustain such an action is a higher standard of proof than that of which the plaintiff or a plaintiff must ordinarily discharge in a civil case).

In June 1980 the plaintiff was examined by a Dr Geraghty a Psychiatrist and Chief Medical Officer of St Columbas Hospital, Sligo administered by the North Western Health Board, who formed the opinion that the plaintiff was suffering from a personality disorder. The doctor then advised the plaintiff's family that they might like a second opinion. The plaintiff then visited a general practitioner in Dublin who felt that the plaintiff's mental disorder had been an isolated condition. He wrote to Dr Geraghty asking for his advices as to what course his treatment should be administered and seeking a case summary from him. Dr Geraghty did not receive the letter until returning home from holidays and admitted in the course of evidence that he had failed to reply to it. Shortly afterwards the plaintiff returned to Sligo. On 19 September 1980, the respondent's wife pursuant to s. 62 of the Act applied to a Dr O'Donnell of Sligo for a recommendation that her husband be received and retained in the District Mental Hospital (St Columbas) as a person of unsound mind. Dr O'Donnell, who was an authorised Medical Officer within the meaning of the Act had examined the respondent in June of that year following complaints by the respondent's wife and he had then concluded that the respondent was a person of unsound mind. After a further examination carried out on the plaintiff the doctor expressed similar opinion and recommended that he should be received and taken under care and treated as a person of unsound mind. He completed the form of recommendation therein and set out his reasons. On arrival at the hospital, the plaintiff was examined by a Dr O'Hare, a member of the hospital staff, who was forced to give the respondent a sedative due to his violent and hostile demeanour. Acting on Dr O'Donnell's recommendation, Dr Geraghty made an order under the provisions of s. 171 that the plaintiff be received and detained in the hospital, although the recommendation under s. 171 should be made by the person who conducted the examination. On 21 September 1980 an application was made under provisions of Article 40 of the Constitution to Barrington J who gave a preliminary order under Article 40.4.2° of the Constitution. The order directed the respondents to produce the applicant in the High Court on 25 September and certify in writing the grounds of his detention. However, by 24 September Dr Geraghty having satisfied himself that the plaintiff had recovered sufficiently discharged him to the care of his brother who had applied for his discharge under s. 220 of the Act. In the High Court the plaintiff sought leave under the provisions of s. 260 of the Act to sue the respondents for damages for assault, battery, and false imprisonment arising out of and incidental to his reception and detention in the psychiatric hospital between 19 and 24 September 1980. In the High Court Costello J gave liberty to the applicant to issue proceedings in the manner requested. Appealed to the Supreme Court.

Held by O'Higgins CJ and Griffin J (Henchy J dissenting)
1. Appeal allowed with the High Court judgment set aside.
2. That there were no substantive grounds for the plaintiff's contention that either Doctor had acted without reasonable care.
3. The use of the word 'satisfied' in the Act indicates that the Oireachtas had in mind a higher standard of proof than that which a plaintiff ordinarily would be required to discharge in a civil case.
4. Henchy J dissenting: that there had been want of care in essential respects. Four of the forms prescribed in the mental treatment regulations constitute an order validating the reception and detention of a person alleged to be of unsound mind and in its form, purpose and effect, that may be compared to a warrant to arrest.
5. All four parts of the prescribed form must be properly completed before a chargeable patient reception order can be said to exist. The evidence deduced is sufficient to show that the defendants, acting vicariously through the Chief Medical Officer of the Hospital, were wanting in reasonable care in the duty owed to the plaintiff.

Cases referred to in judgment
In re Philip Clarke [1950] IR 235
Richardson v London County Council [1957] 1 WLR 751; [1957] 2 All ER 330

Reported at [1983] ILRM 186

In the Matter of the Will of Antonie Marie Bonnet, deceased: Robert William Roche Johnston v Heinz H. Langheld, Kurt Pruessman, Eduard Arthur Seezer and (by order) the Representative Church Body: High Court 1981 No. 312 Sp. (O'Hanlon J) 18 November 1982.

Will - Construction - Testator domiciled abroad - Disposition of immovables - Proper law - Intention of testator - Identity of beneficiary.

Facts The testator was a German national who was at the date of her death and all other material times domiciled in Germany. The will and codicil thereto were in German and contained a bequest of a farm in Ireland to the Protestant Church in Ireland. The deceased and her husband had formed Alfred Bonnet Central Agencies Ltd for the purpose of buying and running a 175 acre farm in Co. Laois. Apart from this farm and the livestock and machinery on it the company only owned a small amount of bank stock and cash in the bank. At the date of her death the testatrix or her nominees held all the shares in the company. The testatrix made her will in haste and the German notary who drafted it did not know what the legal title to the farm was. A special summons for the construction of this bequest was brought which contained two questions: (1) Whether on the true construction of the said will of the said deceased is the aforesaid bequest, a bequest of the shares of the testatrix in Alfred Bonnet Central Agencies Limited? (2) Whether the said bequest was a bequest to the Ministers and members of the Church known as the Lutheran Church in Ireland for the use of the said Church in Ireland? It was contended as a general principle that when a testator is domiciled abroad at the relevant time (which some authors say was the date of the will, and others say is the date of death) the law of the domicile is the law applicable in the construction of the will. The evidence of experts in German law established that the primary principle of construction in the German legal code is that whether or not the case contains a foreign element, a will is to be construed in accordance with the intention of the testator to be gathered from the will.

Held The primary principle of construction in Irish law is the same as that applicable in German law, therefore it was not necessary to determine whether German or Irish law was applicable to the construction of the will. The text of the will was loosely drawn and loosely expressed by the testatrix, and should be construed as referring to her property in Ireland, i.e. the shares in the company. The whole *raison d'etre* of the company was to acquire and run the farm and the testatrix intended to hand over the whole enterprise to the beneficiary. Because of this, and because the parties had agreed at the hearing that the reference in the bequest to the Protestant Church should be identified as referring to the Lutheran Church, both questions in the summons would be answered 'yes'.

Cases referred to in judgment
Re Adams, Deceased [1967] IR 424

Lushington v Sewell (1827) 1 Sim. 435
Re George C. Sillar, Deceased [1956] IR 344
Stewart v Garnett (1830) 3 Sim. 398

Reported at [1983] ILRM 359

Elements in a Theory of Industrial Relations

CHARLES McCARTHY

This book is concerned with law and industrial relations. It does not follow the normal pattern of the debate which appears to have reached a considerable impasse; rather does it attempt to put the questions in a different way. It does this by analysing not merely the law as it stands and applying it to industrial relations but also by exploring a deeper problem — what those engaged in industrial relations believe to be right, to be appropriate, and on the basis of such analysis to identify those rules of conduct which are generally agreed and could well form the basis for law and those rules which carry no such general legitimacy and are doomed to failure. In this way expectations are made clearer, and areas are identified where progress may be made.

Charles McCarthy, MA, PhD, Barrister-at-Law, is Professor of Industrial Relations at Trinity College Dublin, and Dean of the Faculty of Economic and Social Studies.

Is Divorce the Answer?

WILLIAM BINCHY

Ireland is one of the countries which does not have a divorce law, but pressures mount to introduce divorce. In this book William Binchy, a legal expert, examines what has been happening in the area of divorce law world-wide over the past ten years, pointing out the implications for any Irish form of divorce.

William Binchy is a barrister, working as research counsellor with the Law Reform Commission, Dublin. He is an expert in family law, having worked with the Department of Justice from 1974 to 1976 as Special Legal Adviser on family law reform. He has lectured in law at Trinity College Dublin and the University of Dundee. He was Assistant Professor of Law at the University of Ottawa and Visiting Professor at the John Marshall Law School, Chicago.

The Control of Private Rented Dwellings

MARK DE BLACAM

This book describes the present-day Irish law on the control of rented dwellings. The Housing (Private Rented Dwellings) Act, 1982 now forms the basis of control in this area. It grants a measure of security of tenure to the tenants of dwellings controlled under the 1960 and 1967 Acts on rent restriction. In 1983 a further act provided for the terms of tenancies to be fixed by a new body, known as the Rent Tribunal. The book is designed to meet the needs of tenants, property owners and legal practitioners.

Energy and Mineral Resources Law in Ireland

EDWARD DONELAN

This book discusses: The background to onshore and offshore mineral exploration and development in Ireland; The legal basis for exploration (licences) for mines, quarries and wells; Environment protection law; Relevant labour law; State participation, control and regulation.

Edward Donelan, MA, Dip.Eur.Law, Barrister at Law, is a senior draftsman at the office of the Parliamentary Draftsman (Dublin) and author of *The Consumer and the Law* and *Guide to the Sale of Goods and the Supply of Services Act*.

Irish Law Times

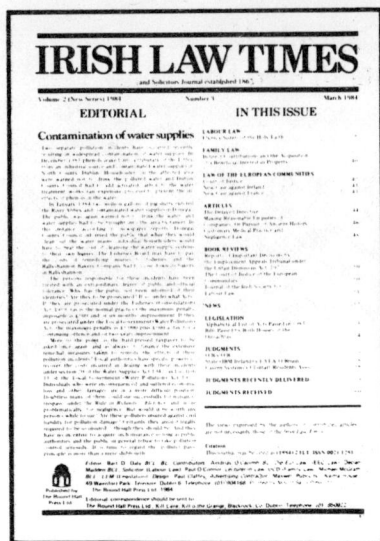

An essential information service for the legal practitioner; surveying bills, acts, case law, with news, profiles and special supplements.

The **Irish Law Times,** which ran from 1867 to 1980, was relaunched in a New Series starting May 1983. The new **Irish Law Times and Solicitors Journal** aims at providing a first-class service to the legal community; it appears in a new format monthly; with emphasis on up-to-date information for the legal profession, regular features on Legislation, Family Law, Labour Law and EEC Law; with news reports, profiles and special supplements on sources of law governing insurance, local government, malicious damage, health and safety, social welfare etc. A Round Hall Press publication.